MY ANCESTO WERE ENGLISH PRESBYTERIANS OR UNITARIANS

HOW CAN I FIND OUT MORE ABOUT THEM?

Alan Ruston

2001

Published by
Society of Genealogists Enterprises Limited
14 Charterhouse Buildings
Goswell Road
London EC1M 7BA
Company Number 3899591

The Society of Genealogists Enterprises Limited is a wholly owned subsidiary
of The Society of Genealogists, a registered charity, no 233701

First edition 1993
Second edition 2001
© Alan Ruston 1993, 2001

ISBN 1 903462 21 5

British Library Cataloguing in Publication Data
A CIP Catalogue record for this book is available from the British Library

About the Author

Alan Ruston is Editor of the *Transactions of the Unitarian Historical Society,*
a trustee of Dr Williams's Library and Chairman of the Herfordshire Record
Society. He was formerly both Chairman of the Hertfordshire Family and
Population History Society and Editor of its journal, *Hertfordshire People.*

CONTENTS

FOREWORD

The appearance of this booklet completed the coverage of the My Ancestor series for what is known as the 'Old English Dissent'. They are the denominations whose origins lie in the religious turbulence of the seventeenth century – the Baptists, the Independents (later Congregationalists), the Presbyterians (the remainder of which mainly became Unitarian) and the Society of Friends – all of whom 'dissented' from the Church of England. In the late seventeenth century the Presbyterians were the largest of the Nonconforming (i.e. from the Church of England) groups, both in terms of numbers of members and chapels. By the early nineteenth century they were the smallest.

The reasons for this decline are many, but need not concern us here, except to point out that many Presbyterian chapels disappeared in the eighteenth century leaving little trace, and their registers disappeared with them. This becomes a difficult problem for the family historian who believes that his or her family had Presbyterian links. However there are ways of tracing these early Presbyterians, and the aim of this work is to provide tools and sources for the researcher to follow up in libraries and record offices. While the chances of success may be limited it would be wrong to paint too bleak a picture. Several former Presbyterian congregations in English county towns commenced keeping registers in the 1690s, which can be examined today at the Public Record Office and in local record offices.

This booklet does not just cover English Presbyterians and Unitarians but also makes mention of the Independents and some of the many varieties of Baptists. This is because denominational boundaries were not always as firmly fixed in the seventeenth and early eighteenth centuries as they later became. Independent and Presbyterian were quite fluid descriptions when applied to many chapels in this period, and so I have attempted to draw a wider canvas. Therefore Geoffrey R Breed's booklet on the Baptists, and D J H Clifford's compilation on the Congregationalists (both in the My Ancestors Were series) should be read in conjunction with this work, as each informs the other in the period up to 1825. After that date denominational boundaries became closely defined and the early fluidity totally disappeared.

I wish to thank Revd Andrew Hill and Dr David Wykes, honorary officers of the Unitarian Historical Society, for their help in the preparation of this booklet. Mr Hill readily updated his lists of chapel record holdings which appear in the Location List, and also kindly looked over the text. I am most grateful to Mrs Sue Kirby who accurately put the whole on a word processor, using amended printed text and handwritten papers that to many would have been indecipherable.

Alan Ruston

Preface to the Second Edition

While the structure of the first edition has in the main been retained, opportunity has been taken to revise and expand the descriptive material. The Location List has been updated where necessary, and explanatory notes have been added.

Perhaps I should clarify at the outset certain of the basic terms used in the text for readers who are unused to the terminology. Dissent describes those denominations, however loosely defined, which arose after 1662, and is considered to consist of the Baptists, the Independents and the English Presbyterians (The Three Denominations). They 'dissented' from the life and work of the Church of England. which was the official church by law established, as it remains today. Sometimes they were called Protestant Dissenters.

Nonconformity on the other hand was a term which became current in the nineteenth century, and described the Three Denominations but also included other organised churches that did not conform to the life and practice of the Church of England. There was a hot debate at certain times as to whether it included the Methodists; it certainly did not include Roman Catholics, and the Quakers/Society of Friends were and are in a class of their own. The term Dissent is only used today in the historical sense, and non-conformity is the universal accepted description of traditional churches within England.

The terms 'chapel', 'church' and 'congregation' are interchangeable terms used to describe individual worshipping groups, although in some circumstances the meanings attached to these words can have wider implications. Before the nineteenth century the overwhelming number of nonconformists met in chapels, never churches as this could confuse them with the established church. The distinction was not a clear one, as the Church of England designated some of their smaller churches as chapels. However over the last hundred years it has become increasingly common to find former nonconformist chapels being designated churches. There is rarely a theological reason for this, but it is a change in social usage of the words. Congregation, on the other hand, describes the group of people who meet in a church or chapel, and distinguishes them from the building in which they meet.

The illustrations are taken from material in my personal collection, with the exception of the title page of the funeral sermon which is used by permission of Dr Williams's Library. I am indebted to Rev. Ann Peart of Withington, Manchester who has revised the Location List for material held in the Manchester area which covers congregations outside Lancashire; she is a noted expert on the extensive holdings of original material held in the Unitarian College Collection, some of which is unlisted.

Alan Ruston *May 2000*

AN OUTLINE HISTORY

Origins

The Reformation in England during the sixteenth century, while turbulent and disruptive, was less violent than in other countries which became Protestant. The group which agitated for a full reformation in the Church, more along European lines and purged of 'Popish practices' became known as the Puritans. The more radical Protestants who cut themselves off from the Church of England, were termed Separatists; they were the spiritual forebears of the Independents, later Congregationalists. The bulk of the Puritans, usually followers of John Calvin, who agitated for reform within the Church of England, became known as Presbyterians. Presbyterianism is a structure of church government, not a system of beliefs, though these English Presbyterians were not organised on a systematic basis.

In 1648 Presbyterianism as a form of church government achieved a brief period of ascendancy. A special treaty between the English Parliamentary party and the Reformed authorities in Scotland made an attempt to introduce 'the word of God and example of the best reformed Churches'. This meant Presbyterianism, probably on the Scottish model for the whole country. This failed for a variety of reasons, and it is probable that only in London, Lancashire and Nottinghamshire were presbyteries set up and even these for only a short time.

With the Restoration of the monarchy in 1660 the Presbyterians, though disliked in the wider community, had hopes of achieving changes in the Church of England to suit their position. However the tide of feeling in the country was against them and others such as the Baptists and the Quakers. It can be said that the old order won the day when in 1662, the Act of Uniformity required, for example, the Book of Common Prayer to be used everywhere. Between 1660 and 1662 about 2,000 clergy were ejected from their livings in the Church for refusing to conform to the Act, and later enactments subjected these often reluctant dissenters to penal penalties if they attempted to live out their faith openly. These events constitute the start of the modern dissenting movement, or as it was later called nonconformity, which has been such a significant feature of English church life.

The Presbyterians were then the largest group in number of members. For many years they were not comfortable as Dissenters and hoped for the opportunity, which never came, of re-entry into the Church of England. The period from 1662 to 1689 was a time of persecution for the Dissenters; they were fined and imprisoned and their meetings, generally held in private houses, had to be held in secret. Some relief was given in 1672 but this was only temporary. This persecution is probably a major reason why there are so few registers or records from this period; if names were recorded in a book which was later seized by the authorities, this was proof before the courts that they belonged to 'an illegal conventicle'.

However it was during this period that the earliest Nonconformist congregations were formed, many of which still continue to this day. There was great fear from the late 1670s that James II and his Roman Catholic ways would lead to greater persecution so there was widespread support amongst Dissenters for William of Orange and Mary when they arrived in 1688. The Toleration Act of 1689 gave them freedom to worship but still kept them out of the mainstream of national life. The next twenty-five years saw an increase in the number of congregations, and of course registers and records, and many Presbyterian congregations, which are now Unitarian, were formed.

Presbyterians and Independents

There appears little to differentiate Presbyterian and Independent churches in the period up to the 1720s. The Presbyterians had no presbytery and each congregation controlled its own affairs. Socially they consisted of the better off amongst the middle classes in town and country, while the Independents, who had always emphasised the separate gathered church, were mainly supported by yeomen and their urban equivalent. However there were no hard and fast distinctions in belief or practice and both were organised on similar principles, a factor of particular importance to family historians. This meant, and continues to mean up to modern times, that each congregation chooses its own officers and committee, determines the worship, selects its own ministers and decides the form, content and structure of the registers and records. Chapel property was, and is, in the hands of individual trustees who often exercise significant local power (the private papers of trustees, where they exist, can be a valuable source about trustees and their activities). There was no external ecclesiastical authority, and associations of congregations as and when formed were loose confederations until the present century. For those Presbyterian (and a very few Independent) congregations, which by 1800 had become Unitarian, this remains the position to the present day.

A consequence of this local autonomy is that no equivalent to bishops' transcripts exists within Dissent. There is no way of reconstructing a lost register from a long defunct congregation. Some Dissenters in the 1690s were doubtful about keeping any records, fearing a return to earlier days of persecution which until the 1720s was always an outside possibility. It was felt by many that ministers should keep personal registers which they took about with them as they moved from congregation to congregation; they were thus not congregational property but could be easily lost amongst personal effects at death.

After Civil Registration came in 1837, individual chapels submitted their original registers to the Registrar-General for retention. They were required to make and retain a copy. This extract is from the copy still in hands of the Stockton-on-Tees Unitarian Chapel, and is an index to the marriages which took place in the late 17th and early 18th centuries. The chapel registers go back to 1688 and the earliest entries were completed by the minister in Latin which is probably unique.

A detailed examination of those chapel registers which have survived (at the Public Record Office in the RG 4 series) shows a distinct lack of uniformity. However the unstructured nature of the entries means that more extensive biographical detail may be shown than was often the case with parish registers. For example the Presbyterian Meeting House, Stockton-on-Tees, now the Unitarian Church, was formed in the summer of 1688, and the first minister Thomas Thompson commenced the register from that date. Some of the early entries are in Latin, but this soon disappeared. Where else would you find the information contained in this entry:

'My dear (& onely own) Brothr John Thompson, was with ye whole ship's company, except one man, cast away on ye coast of Lincolnshire about ye 26 of February 1700/1, ye Lord make me ready also.'

Or even about the Church of England clergy:

'Mr Gibson, ye first Vicar of Stockton (after it was a separate Parish) Died in a feaver on June 17,1714. He came but at May last past, the Lord pity his family, wife & six children (all daughtrs); and provide well for ye Parish.'

The Stockton registers are broadly representative of the records of the period; all the baptisms and marriages (up until 1753 when the Marriage Act prevented further marriages taking place in Dissenting churches) are in the one register covering the period to 1785. The original is in the Public Record Office (PRO RG 4/1097 & 481) with a copy held by the congregation. The Registrar General in accepting registers after 1837 required that a copy be made and these are often to be found amongst local holdings of records. The International Genealogical Index contains entries from dissenting registers lodged with the Registrar General but its necessary uniform format does not allow for the inclusion of the often rich (for family historians) detail that can be found in these early Dissenting registers. It is therefore always wise to look at the original, as it is possible to find so much more.

Presbyterian decline

It has been estimated that in England in 1715 there were some 550 Presbyterian congregations, 300 Independent and 250 Baptist, with upwards of 250,000 attenders. However during the next half century, the number of Dissenting churches which had sprung up in the period to 1710 declined. Many were registered in temporary buildings, like private houses, farms and barns and easily merged with nearby more permanent congregations when the local owner died or lost interest. Others disappeared completely without trace apart from the entry in the chapel licence records, maintained by the local Bishop's court (now to be found in county record offices). In the nineteenth century similar information can be found in returns of places of worship (by county).

The disadvantages of being a Dissenter continued for far longer than many expected, for example restrictions on holding certain public offices, and large numbers of ministers and laity rejoined the Church of England. The biggest decline took place amongst the Presbyterians, who had the greatest hope for an early accommodation with the national church. Being generally of higher social standing amongst the Dissenters

4

CERTIFICATE OF REGISTRY OF THE CHAPEL.

To the Right Reverend Father in God, Bowyer Edward, by Divine permission, Lord Bishop of Chester.

We, whose names are hereunto subscribed, being his Majesty's Protestant subjects, dissenting from the Church of England, have agreed to set apart for the public worship of Almighty God, a certain edifice or building (newly erected) situate at Renshaw Street, in Liverpool, in the county of Lancaster and diocese of Chester, called or known by the name of the "Presbyterian Chapel or Meeting-house," and desire that the same may be registered according to an Act of Parliament made in the first year of the reign of their late Majesties King William and Queen Mary, intitled, "An Act for exempting their Majesties' Protestant Subjects dissenting from the Church of England from the Penalties of certain Laws."

Witness our hands this sixteenth day of October, in the year of our Lord One thousand, eight hundred and eleven.

Robert Lewin, minister of the said chapel.

Thomas Holt,	Thomas Mather,
Thomas Thornely,	Thomas Booth,
Henry Ellison,	John Swanwick,
Thomas Bolton,	William Jevons.
John R. Freme,	

The 18th day of October, 1811. Registered in the Public Episcopal Registry at Chester, according to the Act above mentioned.

William Ward, Deputy Registrar.

All dissenting chapels had to be registered with the local Bishops court. Certificates vary widely but this one from Liverpool was legally drawn up and includes all the essential elements. The state took over chapel registration from the Bishops courts in the mid-19th Century.

5

and less sectarian in outlook, their members were keen to become part of the life of the parish church. These factors, combined with theological turbulence, led many to leave and join the Church, which accentuated the decline. However, in London in the eighteenth century, the leading Presbyterian congregations contained some very wealthy supporters who maintained ministers of a high calibre. Congregations were maintained by subscription and pew rents and only those who subscribed in some way were members who could take part in the running of the chapel.

Family historians may find references in contemporary papers to congregations of this period to which an ancestor may have belonged that cannot be located in the more precise records of a later date. Unfortunately in the vast majority of cases this is likely to be the end of the matter. Unless the registers, if indeed they existed in the first place, were incorporated or associated with those of a neighbouring Dissenting congregation (either Presbyterian or Independent), then there is no other extant source to locate details about individuals who had been members.

There are, however, published sources which list the names of the leading figures of many congregations that disappeared in the early eighteenth century. G Lyon Turner's *Original Records of early Nonconformity under persecution and indulgence* (3 vols., London, 1911), lists hundreds of names of people connected with Presbyterian, Independent and Baptist churches as well as early Quaker meeting houses in the period 1660s-1680s. Volume 2 (1,348 pages) provides a detailed index, which includes alphabetical lists of teachers and householders who supported applications for chapel licences. Joseph Hunter, Familiae Minorium Gentium (4 vols., *Harleian Society,* 1894 and 1936), also provides useful detail on leading families. Two other books list names of Presbyterians of this period (though chiefly of ministers or preachers), both by Alexander Gordon - *Freedom After Ejection* (Manchester, 1917), and *Cheshire Classis Minutes 1691-1745* (London, 1919). B Nightingale, *Lancashire Nonconformity* (6 vols., 1893), is an indispensable guide to Congregational and Presbyterian churches in this period and later, and does contain material of interest to the family historian.

Presbyterianism becomes Unitarianism

This booklet does not need to describe the various theological changes which took place in English Dissent during the eighteenth and nineteenth centuries. There are many works on this complex subject, and some are listed in the Bibliography for those who wish to learn what their ancestor's religious beliefs may have been. It will be sufficient to state that Unitarianism (also called Socinianism) arose because an increasing number of people refused to believe in the Trinity (Father, Son and Holy Spirit) which lies at the centre of the Christian creeds. The seventeenth-century religious establishment held that those who denied the Biblical basis of the Trinity endangered the foundations of Christian belief, so much so that even the Toleration Act of 1689 refused to accord them toleration. However the eighteenth century was a period of philosophical and spiritual doubt within both the Church of England and in Dissent, so that the question of the validity of the Trinity became one of the key issues of theological dispute.

English Presbyterianism embraced the new philosophical climate, and by the 1790s most members of these congregations had become Unitarian (or Arian) in belief. Before 1813 the open avowal of anti-Trinitarianism was illegal, so the Presbyterian name was retained for the meeting houses, although individuals often called themselves Radical or Rational Dissenters, or Unitarians. This theological ferment came at roughly the same time as the arrival of Methodism. These two seemingly opposing trends within Christianity (one based on a belief in rationality and the other on enthusiasm and justification by faith) revolutionised the English religious scene. Revolutionary is perhaps the key word to describe the period. The American Revolution was strongly supported by many Dissenters. The French Revolution was viewed initially by most Rational Dissenters as an exciting development (before it became violent) with the hope that at least some of the changes might come to England. This caused a backlash amongst the more orthodox Dissenters and in society at large, so that Unitarians became generally disliked and distrusted. Many left to go to America, including its formative leader Joseph Priestley.

Family historians should remember that from the 1790s the old Presbyterian churches, which had declined in number when compared with the Independents or Baptists, became clearly separate from the other Dissenting churches with whom they formerly had close connections. Welsh-speaking Unitarianism grew at this time, mainly concentrated in Carmarthenshire. It was termed the 'black spot' by other denominations in Wales in the nineteenth century. Disputes were bitter and over most of England and Wales assertive denominationalism was becoming the rule.

The General Baptists

Family historians may be surprised to see the inclusion of Baptists in this present booklet. G Breed, in his *My ancestors were Baptists*, in quoting from the Baptist Union Directory, explains that a 'New Connection' of the more evangelical General Baptists was formed in 1770, under the influence of the Methodist revival. Other General Baptist churches decided not to join this movement, and many of these congregations became Unitarian.

7

The General Baptist Assembly was formed in 1653. By the late eighteenth century many of its oldest member churches, mainly centred in the south-east of England, had been affected by the Unitarian thinking of the period whilst retaining the practices of Baptists. The creation of the New Connection attracted churches away from the Assembly, with those who remained becoming ever closer to Presbyterian/Unitarian thinking. In 1915 an arrangement was made so that the majority of churches in the Assembly should join the Unitarians, and a minority the Baptist Union. The former group, while today classed as Unitarian Churches, maintain the General Baptist Assembly (whose records are in Dr Williams's Library). The registers and minute books of these churches are generally in excellent condition and provide much detail especially on baptisms and discipline. Those situated in Sussex have been transcribed, and copies are in Dr Williams's Library. A history of the life and work of this unique community in Sussex is available (John Caffyn, *Sussex Believers: Baptist marriages in the seventeenth and eighteenth centuries,* Churchman Publishing, 1988). Inter-marriage between member families went on for generations with the same names constantly re-occurring.

The denominational setting

Bitter theological dispute and rivalry between Dissenting churches took place from about 1812 and in the next twenty years denominational structures were formed – the Baptist Union (of Particular Baptists) in 1812, the British and Foreign Unitarian Association in 1825, and the Congregational Union (of Independent Churches) in 1831. It was also the period when the last civil disabilities suffered by Dissenters were removed. Whilst in these developments we see the beginnings of modern Nonconformity, the change is of little significance to family historians. The attitude towards records did not change and no rules on their nature and retention were issued. The importance accorded to the preservation of church papers remained low. The foundation of the Historical Societies within the denominations after 1900 was partly an attempt to change attitudes in this area.

The new central organisations were singularly ineffective – few congregations belonged to them and the old denominational titles were maintained. Of the congregations who lodged their registers after 1837 a few were stated to be Unitarian; this was due, not only to the tradition that sought to retain the Presbyterian or General Baptist name, but also legal disputes on the legality of Unitarianism before 1813. The legal tangles dragged on until 1844 when the passing of the Dissenters' Chapels Act secured for the Unitarians the ownership of their buildings. The position is made more complex by the foundation of Presbyterian Churches of the Scottish type in England at roughly the same time, often in the northern counties, with synodical government and a different theology. These were grouped together into the Presbyterian Church of England formed in 1836. This new body claimed its members had taken over the rights and privileges of the English Presbyterians who had 'disappeared' into Unitarianism.

All this makes it very difficult for the family historian who sees 'Presbyterian' against the entry of Registers deposited at the General Register Office after 1837. Others are shown as 'Independent/Presbyterian' or 'formerly Presbyterian'. As a broad rule of thumb congregations formed before 1790 are almost certain to be English Presbyterian (and by 1837 generally Unitarian in fact, if not in name). The name has clung on in certain places so, for example, Hyde Chapel, Gee Cross, nr. Stockport, Cheshire (founded in 1708), while Unitarian in affiliation, retains as its denominational title Presbyterian.

The recent story

The history of the denominations since 1850 is of limited interest to the family historian. Civil registration was seen as a triumph for Nonconformity and for the Unitarians in particular, whose objection to the Church of England marriage service was a prime cause for the change. Attitudes towards the keeping of records by the congregations were as mixed as ever and attempts at standardisation of registers met with little success. The state was doing the job now. Why, therefore, should Nonconformity carry out the role especially as it was only taking over the task of the Church of England, which many felt should (and would before long) become disestablished?

Independent churches slowly came to call themselves Congregational, while Unitarians often went straight from terming their chapels 'Presbyterian' to that of 'Free Christian' for theological reasons, but remaining members of the Unitarian body. It is difficult to see the three branches of the Old Dissent as being churches in the same sense as the Anglican and Roman Catholic Churches. Unitarian churches remain to this day totally congregational in polity, despite the formation in 1929 of the General Assembly of Unitarian and Free Christian Churches to which all belong. The Congregational Union was always a loose confederation of churches, which did not change until it joined with the Presbyterian Church of England and the Churches of Christ to form the United Reformed Church in 1972. The Baptist Union has never exercised denominational authority over individual congregations, and in the view of some, is always about to split apart. None of this seemingly chaotic structure, of which this is only a skeleton outline, aids those family historians with a passionate interest in their Dissenter ancestor but not in the chapel background and organisation.

SOURCES OF INFORMATION

Registers

Up to 1720, all Dissenters feared a return to times of persecution, and were much relieved when the Protestant Hanoverians come to the British throne in 1714. They avoided accumulating written 'evidence' of their Dissent that could be used in the courts if the repression returned. Therefore registers mentioning members are few and then often the personal property of the minister who took them from place to place; a personal record was not likely to be admissible in court. While the Presbyterian (the name was retained to affirm a belief in the importance of an educated ministry, i.e. presbyters, not the system of organisation) minister was in the main of a higher educational level than that of other Dissenters, it does not mean that they kept more and better registers. The disinclination to create and maintain records, while not universal, was general and became ingrained, to the loss of the genealogist. While marriages and burials may have taken place in the parish church, most Dissenting baptisms took place either at home or in the chapel. They were often not recorded in the parish registers.

The registers come in all shapes and sizes, as do the membership and minute books which can contain information of interest to the family historian. Some have baptisms, marriages and burials all in one book while others are kept separately. A good example is Rivington Presbyterian Chapel in Lancashire, where inside the one volume is written:

> 'Rivington Chapel
> Rejistar of Births 1747-1891
> Rejistar of Burials 1817-1891'

The register has been transcribed (published 1988) by J Holding and C D Rogers who bring out its chaotic nature. When the congregation presented the volume to the Registrar General in 1838 it was rejected (but partially accepted in 1858) as much had been entered long after the recorded event. The transcribers conclude:

> 'The reason for the rejection is that whereas, from 1820, the entries of baptism are, with few exceptions, presented in chronological order, those dated earlier appear to have no rational sequence, and therefore cannot have been compiled in the normal way, i.e. data being entered at the time of the ceremony concerned. Moreover entries for the first forty years and more appear to be in the same handwriting, with the exception of some interpolated entries. Rivington was not alone in receiving a rebuff from the Commissioners; some congregations, which had apparently not been in the practice of keeping a written record, compiled entries in 1837/8 specifically for the purpose.'

Many volumes must have been rejected on this basis, and you will note in the Location List to this booklet that there are several congregations of seventeenth and eighteenth century foundation who are not shown as submitting registers. They may have been rejected as defective, but they would be very valuable today to the family historian. This example shows how in 1837/38 certain congregations of all denominations wrote up their records long after the event so the accuracy can, in some cases, be open to question.

Other Records

Subscription and communicant books from the eighteenth century and membership lists from about 1810 onwards can prove invaluable in tracing ancestors, if not always giving exact genealogical detail. There are also bound volumes of various types which can contain varied and valuable detail on people. For example at Stockton the subscription book for 1773 is the only source that exists from which the late eighteenth century membership can be determined. In other places, the address of members is given (rarely date of birth), and the date of death or cessation of membership. In instances of removal from the area the new address in village or town may be given.

In General Baptist churches, and possibly in certain Presbyterian churches though I have never seen an example, there are discipline books up to about 1780. They record occasions when congregations, in small and rather close rural communities, ejected or suspended members for misdemeanours, where the 'turning away' or 'withdrawing' as it was often called had a real impact on the individual. The most notable example I have seen is the Memorandum/discipline book of the Old Meeting House (General Baptist) at Ditchling Sussex, covering the period 1753-1803. Most family historians would be delighted to find an entry for an ancestor like the following:

'18 May 1757. The case of John Vincent was Considered and whereas he has been Admonished several times and has Promised a Reformation, but still Remains in a Carles(sic) way and sildom goes to any hearing of a Sunday and Follows Gaming and keeping of bad Company and Breaks his promise in Regard to making good his Payments, therefore we agree to withdraw from him for such Disorderly Walking.'

RULES

UNITARIAN FUND,

ESTABLISHED 1806.

TO WHICH ARE ADDED

A STATEMENT OF THE SOCIETY'S ACCOUNTS,

AND

A LIST OF SUBSCRIBERS,

&c. &c.

FOR 1813 AND 1814.

PRINTED BY C. STOWER, BROOKSBY'S WALK

1814.

This early list of rules and subscribers in particular is one that could be of interest to Family Historians. Like other lists it contains a long list of names, sometimes with addresses.

There are riches for the family historian not only in the registers but in the other records of the congregation if an ancestor can be shown to be associated with it. Where registers cannot establish a firm connection, it is possible that other contemporary documents could provide important information. This is made easier as ever increasing quantities of records of Dissenting congregations are lodged in record offices and made more widely available by other means.

Dr Williams's Library Register of Births (now at the Public Record Office)

A record of births amongst Dissenters from 1742 was maintained at Dr Williams's Library (run by the trust created on the founder's death in 1716 which became the main repository of dissenting books and records in London). The Library attempted to create an authoritative source for the registration of births to Dissenting families to overcome legal difficulties for those births not recorded as baptisms in parish registers. The Register was more a hope for the future as the courts at that time, and for long after, refused to accept the legality of Dissenting registers. The aim was also to make up for the deficiencies amongst ministers who were often lax record keepers.

Known as the Protestant Dissenters' register, it was open nationally to parents ready to sign a certificate of their child's birth and to spend 6 pence (later increased to 1 shilling) for registration. Parents had to produce two parchment certificates signed by the local minister and midwife and one or two of those present at the birth giving the name, sex, parents and place (street, parish, county) of birth. After 1828 paper certificates were required in addition to the signature of both parents. The details were then entered into a register, with one certificate being retained (now at the PRO in RG5) and the other returned to the parents with a certificate of registration.

By 1769 less than 400 entries had been made in the Register (some were for births before 1742), but the number had increased to over a thousand by 1780. From the late eighteenth century onwards the number of registrations increased considerably especially as ministers were permitted to lodge birth details. It was a laborious process only likely to be undertaken by the more educated and affluent of the dissenters. Often whole families were registered together, some many years after their birth.When civil registration commenced in 1837 the Register consisted of nearly 49,000 birth entries, which was handed over in its entirety to the Registrar General. They can now be consulted in the PRO (not at Dr Williams's Library which holds no details or papers relating to the Register) and there is a form of index. A photocopy in several bound volumes of the Register is to found in the public search room at the PRO at Kew.

The Family Connection

It has often been said that the history of Dissent is that of families, whose tentacles reach out over several chapels and sometimes across denominational boundaries. Families remain associated with specific chapels over very long periods of time, sometimes hundreds of years. For example the descendants of William Evershed and other families who founded the General Baptist Chapel at Billingshurst, Sussex, in 1740 remain members of the congregation up to the present. It was said of the Ridge family of Westgate (Presbyterian) Chapel, Lewes, and elsewhere in Sussex, up until the mid-nineteenth century, 'assembled not only to worship but also to meet each other'. If the family historian can find a forebear from one of these Disssenting families, which generally consisted of both rich and poor, then they may have found a very rich seam in which to dig.

The family associations can be seen from the monumental inscriptions found in the burial grounds attached to older chapels. Members of a particular family were often interred in one area of the yard, and associated gravestones can show the extent of inter-marriage over generations. Records of monumental inscriptions, some recorded in the nineteenth century, can be a useful tool for the family historian in sorting out complex relationships.

Records from the nineteenth and twentieth centuries often consist of minutes of annual and committee meetings (sometimes printed), membership books, financial records of all types as well as letterbooks and documents. Church calendars can be an invaluable source when an ancestor has been positively located to a particular congregation; a recognisable form of calendar may be found from the 1870s onwards. Sunday schools, and up to the 1860s day schools for the poor were often large and had their own extensive documentation. These can provide ages and possibly the names of parents where other sources are silent. Miscellaneous books, and references in calendars are to be found amongst congregational records referring to those who were killed or served in the First World War.

Repositories of material

Apart from holdings in record offices all over the country shown in the Location List, there are three major libraries which contain material of use to the family historian. These are not places to start out on your researches, and should only be contacted when a specific reference to a known ancestor needs to be followed up. It is no use asking these libraries to help with a query such as 'I want to find out about John Taylor who may have been a dissenter in the London area about 1850'. This will draw a total blank unless he happened to be a leading figure or a minister. It is essential to know the name and exact location of the chapel and the denomination with which an ancestor was connected before starting to look for local chapel records.

For those with distinguished Nonconformist ancestors in London, the records of Bunhill Row burial ground (up to 1855) could be a useful starting point. *The Dictionary of National Biography,* and the *New Dictionary of National Biography* when it appears, contains many references to the leading Nonconformists, particularly ministers. For the more ordinary church member, it will be necessary to know the name of the chapel to which they are likely to have belonged. From there further detail may become available though it will almost certainly be necessary to go to record repositories and possibly contact the local congregation to locate the original records.

Dr Williams's Library, 14 Gordon Square, London, WC1H OAG (telephone 020 7387 3727)

The Library is mentioned in most books on genealogy and family history, but little detail is usually given as to its holdings. Most of its books and manuscripts concern the history of the Old Dissent, and is particularly strong on English Presbyterians, Unitarians and the Congregationalists. The Congregational Library, formerly at the Memorial Hall in London, is now housed at Gordon Square as a separate collection. The Library has no original material on Methodism, Quakerism or denominations formed after 1850. There are printed catalogues of library holdings. The following sources within the collection are likely to be of value to the family historian:

Chapel histories. The Library has perhaps the most comprehensive collection in the country which is constantly being added to by donation and purchase. *Nonconformist Congregations in GB; a list of histories and other materials held in Dr Williams's Library*, published in 1973 shows how rich and unique is the collection. This book, which is to be found in many reference libraries, is currently under revision as much material has been subsequently added.

Surman Index. This large card index gives biographical information and references on Dissenting ministers from the seventeenth century to the 1960s, compiled by the late Revd C E Surman. It is primarily of Independent/Congregational ministers, but includes some Presbyterian/Unitarians and a small number of Baptists. It is not comprehensive and its best coverage is of those ministers who went to a theological college. It is currently being updated to include twentieth century Congregational/URC ministers and others.

THE

WISDOM AND BENEVOLENCE OF

𝕿𝖍𝖊 𝕯𝖊𝖎𝖙𝖞

IN THE ORDINATION OF DEATH:

A DISCOURSE,

OCCASIONED BY THE DEATH

OF

THE REV. THOMAS HOWE,

𝕯𝖊𝖑𝖎𝖛𝖊𝖗𝖊𝖉 𝖆𝖙 𝕭𝖗𝖎𝖉𝖕𝖔𝖗𝖙,

NOVEMBER 26ᴛʜ, 1820.

BY

T. SOUTHWOOD SMITH, M.D.

𝕷𝖔𝖓𝖉𝖔𝖓:

PUBLISHED BY SHERWOOD, NEELY AND JONES,
PATERNOSTER ROW.

1821.

The front page of a funeral sermon - some can contain useful biographical background.

Denominational journals. It has runs of most of the publications from the eighteenth century to date (*see* later section).

Manuscripts. The Library has a large collection of letters and early lists of congregations, e.g. the Evans List 1715 and the Thompson List 1773, but manuscripts are not a useful source for the family historian unless the researcher is looking for detail on a well-known figure. There are also some holdings of original chapel records, but the majority of these are of limited genealogical use. A brief published guide to the manuscripts is available but this is in outline form only.

Funeral Sermons. From the seventeenth to the mid-nineteenth century, funeral sermons were often published and the Library has a large holding. They chiefly concern leading figures, i.e. ministers and rich laypeople, and contain much contemporary theology now of little relevance. Sometimes there are nuggets of valuable biographical information to be found in these sermons, and should not be ignored by the family historian.

Autobiographies/biographies. Published books from the nineteenth and twentieth centuries may contain recollections about an ancestor, but this source is only likely to be useful to the family historian if a connection with a well-known figure is clearly established.

The Library staff will give as much help as they can to family historians but their main task is servicing the needs of scholars and academics researching theology, philosophy and the history of Dissent. It is a private, not a public library, with membership by subscription. It does not carry out genealogical research. While casual callers will be attended to if at all possible it would be wise to telephone prior to a proposed visit, or to write. The Library is open 10.00 to 17.00 Monday, Wednesday and Friday, and to 18.30 on Tuesday and Thursday.

John Rylands University Library of Manchester, Deansgate, Manchester M3 3EH

The Library has long been known as a chief repository for Methodist archives, but it also has extensive holdings relating to the other Dissenting denominations. Apart from the Surman Index, the material held is similar to that of Dr Williams's Library, though there are greater holdings on Nonconformity in the north of England. There are 28,000 books and pamphlets, 4,000 periodical volumes and 43,000 manuscripts on Presbyterians and Unitarians, although only a small proportion of these would interest the family historian. Most of this material was transferred to the Library from the Unitarian College Manchester Collection. Arrangements to visit the Library should be made through the Special Collections Division. For a general description of holdings see C D Field, *Sources for the Study of Protestant Nonconformity in John Rylands etc,* (reprinted from the Library Bulletin, Summer 1989).

Harris Manchester College Library, Mansfield Road, Oxford OX1 3TD

Harris Manchester College is a college of the University of Oxford, and access to its Library is by prior arrangement only. Fomerly Manchester College it was founded in 1786 in Manchester, with later periods in York and London, to train dissenting ministers and laymen of the Presbyterian tradition. The College has, and continues to have, strong connections with English Presbyterianism/Unitarianism about which it has a large collection of books and manuscripts. A catalogue to the latter has been published (Dennis Porter, *A Catalogue of the Manuscripts in Harris Manchester College Oxford,* Oxford, 1998). The major interest for the family historian however is the Johnston Index. This extensive slip index (approximately 25,000 slips) is alphabetical and lists all the obituaries that have appeared in Unitarian and related journals from 1794 to date. While it only gives the name, the journal date and reference, the index makes it possible to trace biographical details of some quite minor figures within Unitarianism. The only copy is at Oxford though there are plans to make it more widely available. The number of Unitarians in the UK has not exceeded 60,000 at any one time and this unique index was compiled over many years. It would be an almost impossible task for the much larger Congregational or Baptist denominations whose extensive obituaries in journals are unindexed.

Contact with the College is by post only to the Librarian, and the Library staff are willing to consult the index for specific names in return for an SAE and a small donation to College funds.

The United Reformed Church History Society

Westminster College, Cambridge CB3 0AA, phone 01223 741084, holds archive material for this Society on some early English Presbyterian churches which by about 1800 had become Independent rather than Unitarian. It also holds mainly nineteenth century records of constituent churches of the Presbyterian Church of England, founded in 1836, that became part of the United Reformed Church in 1972, and which should not be confused with English Presbyterianism which can be said to have disappeared by 1840, though often not in name.

Journals and newspapers

Entries for births, marriages and deaths in newspapers are one of the key sources for the family historian. Local and national newspapers can be searched diligently but mostly with little success unless dates and places are precisely known. It is also disappointing to note that, except for the great and good, newspaper obituaries as we know them today did not really appear before the 1850s. But this cannot be said about the religious journals which were particularly strong in this respect from about 1800 onwards.

The recognisable denominational newspaper first appeared in the 1790s and by 1815, with heightened Dissenting consciousness, their number had burgeoned in all the denominations. Some only lasted for short periods. There were few marriages entries and hardly any births because, in the main, inclusion was determined by the editor and it was obituaries which created the chief interest. By the 1840s however the papers' owners had found a valuable source of income in publishing personal notices so separate sections were created to meet this demand. After 1837 marriages could take place in Dissenting chapels and this 'novelty' meant that for the next five years or so they were extensively reported. In some cases they include almost as much detail as the marriage certificate.

However it is for the period before civil registration that these journals and newspapers will be of significant interest to the family historian. Obituaries of leading figures always appeared but also some very ordinary or poor people were noted who had 'died well in the faith'. Dissenting obituaries in this period can strike an amusing note for the modern reader though others may find them depressing and repetitive. They did not vary much across the denominations except in the theological gloss that was included. Their length and candour are a boon to the researcher, though some of them are infuriatingly deficient in important facts. Sometimes there is great detail about the deceased but for example their age at death, or for married women their first name, is omitted. While men preponderate, a significant number of women are included; an analysis of the *Monthly Repository* for the period 1806-32 shows that over 27% were obituaries of women.

This is an extract from one of the most informative:

'Died, March 22nd 1816, in her 52nd year, Ann, wife of Mr.Robert Blyth, of Birmingham (to who she was married April 10,1783), and daughter of the late Mr.George Brittain, merchant, of Sheffield... Her estimable and liberal-minded parents, had educated her to the principles of the Established Church. The events, however of her early life, led her to examine the foundation of Unitarian Dissent....she saw reason to embrace that simple faith in the evidences and obligations of which she assiduously instructed her children; ten out of the eleven, of who survive to bless her memory etc.' (*Monthly Repository*, April 1816, p 242/3)

D J Steel, *National Index of Parish Registers, Vol II: Sources for Nonconformist genealogy and family history* (2002), mentions only three short-lived Unitarian periodicals. There were many more than this, and the following is a list of periodicals which are known to include entries of births, marriages and deaths. Those marked with an * have been used to create the Johnston Index held at Harris Manchester College Oxford, and those with an + appear in my publication, *Unitarian obituaries 1794-1850, Index & synopsis* (1990). The dates given are the first and last year of the journals' publication:

*+   *Protestant dissenters magazine,* 1794-99
*+   *Universalists miscellany/universal theological magazine,* 1797-1805
*   *Monthly repository, 1806-38* (no obituaries after 1832)
*+   *Christian reformer,* 1815-63
+   *Christian reflector* (Liverpool), 1820-29
+   *Christian pioneer* (Glasgow), 1826-45
+   *Unitarian chronicle,* 1832-35
+   *Gospel advocate* (General Baptist), 1833-37
+   *General Baptist news,* 1831-36
+   *Unitarian Baptist advocate,* 1837-39
*   *The inquirer,* 1842 – still in publication. The oldest dissenting newspaper still in existence, it provides the bulk of the notices.
      Yr ymfynnydd (Welsh language), 1847 – still in publication.
+   *The Unitarian,* 1846
      Unitarian herald, 1861-8
+   *The Christian life,* 1876-1929
      The Unitarian, 1903 (founded as The Unity) – monthly, still in publication.

Sept. 16, Mr. JOHN FRANKLAND of Leeds, aged 66 years.

September 22, at her mother's house, Broughton, near Manchester, in the 49th year of her age, ELIZABETH TREMLETT, sole surviving daughter of the late Rev. William JOHNS. A cultivated mind, blended with a gentle and tender spirit, and a thoughtful consideration for others' happiness, gave value and interest to an existence, whose brightness had been overcast by the languor of disease and the sorrow of domestic bereavements, and whose premature termination has left regrets and affectionate remembrances in the hearts of many friends.

Sept. 29, at Lane Foot, near Kendal, after a decline of several years, aged 37, JANE, the wife of the Rev. EDWARD HAWKES.

October 2, at her house, Derby Terrace, Nottingham, in the 74th year of her age, ELIZABETH, relict of the Rev. James TAYLER, formerly one of the pastors of the High-Pavement society of Protestant Dissenters in that town. Uniting strong affections with an excellent understanding and great energy of purpose, her children have lost in her a most devoted parent, and all who needed help a generous and sympathizing friend.

Oct. 2, at Merthyr Tydvil, aged 18 years, ELINOR, the eldest daughter of Mr. Thomas JONES. "Indeed, it is hard to say that it is all well."

Lately, at Bangor (N. A.), aged 82 years, Rev. WILLIAM MASON. He was born at Princeton, Mass., and graduated at Harvard College in 1792. In 1798, he was ordained as pastor of the Congregational church in Castine, Me., of which place he was the first, and for many years the only minister. In 1834, he resigned his ministry and removed to Bangor, where he resided till his death. He was one of the first clergymen, in that part of the state, to bear the reproach of Unitarian opinions, a reproach which did not disturb his equanimity nor weaken his kindness and charity for those who bestowed it. He was distinguished by sincerity and openness of character, gentleness of disposition, and uniform cheerfulness.

MARRIAGES.

1847. Aug. 29, at the Old St. Nicholas chapel, by Rev. T. F. Thomas, Mr. AUGUSTUS W. SCOPES to Miss MARY ROBINSON, of Ipswich.

Sept. 19, at the chapel in the Conigree, Trowbridge, by Rev. S. Martin, Mr. ISAAC ALLEN to Miss MARY GIBSON.

Sept. 19, at Bank-Street chapel, Bol-

ANN GOODIER, both of Hale, near Altrincham.

Oct. 5, at the chapel in the Conigree, Trowbridge, by Rev. Samuel Martin, Mr. JAMES BRINKWORTH to Miss JANE BOUCHER.

Oct. 7, in London, JOHN PHIPSON, Esq., of Edgbaston, Birmingham, to ELIZA, youngest daughter of the late Joseph Powell, Esq., of Exeter

This comes from the monthly Unitarian journal, 'The Christian Reformer'. Its real interest for family Historians is obvious.

In addition to the printed extraction mentioned above, I published a booklet *Monthly repository 1806-1832: Index and synopsis of the obituaries* (1985). In both my publications the full name, journal and page reference, place and date of death and age are recorded. Both are now out of print but can be consulted in numerous libraries.

The Unitarian year book, under various names, can be an important tool for the family historian from the 1860s onwards. This not only gives details of each congregation, but lists all the ministers with their addresses. From 1890, obituaries of deceased ministers appear plus names of church officers. These books were published under the following names:

> *British and Irish Unitarian Almanack,* 1847-51
> *The Unitarian Almanac,* 1852-64
> *The Unitarian Pocket Almanac,* 1864-?1900
> *The Essex Hall Year Book,* 1890-1928
> *Unitarian & Free Christian Churches Year Book,* 1929 – continuing until the
> 1980s when it was renamed the *Directory and Handbook.*

Many of the earlier volumes are very rare, and whilst the libraries already mentioned hold partial runs, it is understood that the British Library has almost a complete set. An index to the obituaries of Unitarian ministers who died in the period 1900-1999 is found in a supplement to the *Transactions of the Unitarian Historical Society* April 2000, and can be purchased as a separate item. The *Transactions* which first appeared in 1916 is the main journal for the publication of articles on British Unitarian history. Past issues can be seen in libraries and information about current issues can be obtained from Dr Williams's Library.

BIBLIOGRAPHY

a. General history

Watts, M, *The dissenters, from the reformation to the French revolution* (Oxford University Press, 1978), is the most widely available work on the history of the Old Dissent to 1790 (now in paperback). *The dissenters, Volume 2: The expansion of evangelical nonconformity 1791-1859,* Oxford, 1995 is possibly not as valuable for the general reader. D Coomer, *English dissent under the early Hanoverians* (London, 1946) is a shorter work covering the period up to 1750. Unfortunately this excellent introductory book has long been out of print.

Briggs, John, and Ian Sellers, *Victorian nonconformity,* London, 1973, and David Thompson, *Nonconformity in the nineteenth century,* London, 1972, provide a flavour of the period of expansion through extracts from centemporary documents. David Shorney, *Protestant nonconformity and Roman Catholicism,* a guide to the sources in the PRO, PRO Readers Guide No 13, 1996 is a useful introduction for the family historian. The glossary and bibliography are useful but it is weak on the Presbyterian/Unitarian records and background.

There are few general histories of the English Presbyterians/Unitarians. C G Bolam, Goring, Short and Thomas, *The English Presbyterians: from Elizabethan Puritanism to modern Unitarianism* (London, 1968) is a long scholarly work. A simpler and more popular treatment is to be found in J and R Goring, *The Unitarians* (Wheaton Christian Denominations Series, Exeter, 1984). The most detailed listing available of churches that are known to have existed since the seventeenth century can be found in *The Unitarian Heritage,* an architectural survey of chapels and churches in the Unitarian tradition in the British Isles, ed. G and J Hague (Sheffield, 1986). The *Transactions of the Unitarian Historical Society,* issued at least yearly from 1916, contain articles on English Presbyterians and Unitarians and their churches from the seventeenth to the twentieth century.

Turner, G Lyon, *Original records of early nonconformity under persecution and indulgence,* 3 vols, London, 1911-1914; Joseph Hunter, *Familiae Minorium Gentium,* 4 vols, Harleian Society, London, 1894 and 1936; B Nightingale, *Lancashire Nonconformity,* 6 vols, 1893, and Alexander Gordon's, *Freedom after ejection,* Manchester, 1917 and *Cheshire Classis Minutes 1691-1745,* London, 1919 are described in the text.

Works covering specific areas of interest:

Caffyn, John, *Sussex believers: baptist marriages in the seventeenth and eighteenth centuries,* Churchman Publishing, 1988

Field, C D, *Sources for the study of protestant nonconformity in John Rylands etc,* reprinted from the Library Bulletin, Summer 1989

Porter, D, *A catalogue of manuscripts in Harris Manchester College Oxford,* Oxford, 1998.

Murch, J, *The History of the presbyterian and general baptist churches in the west of England,* London, 1835.

Ramsden, G M, *A responsible society,* 1985. Gives biographical details of leading families for Bolton, Bank Street Chapel.

Urwick, W, *Nonconformity in Chester,* London, 1864.

Urwick, W, *Nonconformity in Hertfordshire,* London 1884.

Wilson, W, *History of dissenting churches and meeting houses in London,* 4 Vols, 1808-1814.

Nonconformist congregations in GB; a list of histories and other materials held in Dr Williams's Library, London, 1973 (under revision)

b. Sources and works for the family historian

Mullett, M, *Sources for the History of English Nonconformity 1660-1830* (British Records Association, London, 1991), describes in general terms the records of the General Baptists, Particular Baptists, Independents, Methodists, Presbyterians and Unitarians, Society of Friends and other smaller churches like the the Moravians and Muggletonians. The book gives many examples of entries taken from registers and other records that will be of interest to the family historian. However it is written for the general researcher and only gives partial lists of holdings in record offices. It has a valuable bibliography.

Steel, D J, *National Index of Parish Registers, Vol II: Sources for Nonconformist Genealogy and Family History,* (SoG 2001), affords a very valuable survey and remains an excellent descriptive account of the registers and other records of the various denominations.

Palgrave-Moore, P, *Understanding the history and records of Nonconformity* (Norwich, 1988), is easily available to family historians. It is a brave attempt to cover the whole field in just a few pages.

Gandy, Michael, *Basic facts about English Nonconformity for family historians* (Federation of Family History Societies 1998) is even briefer but has a firm grasp of the main features of nonconformist history.

c. Useful lists

The List of Non-Parochial registers and records in the custody of the Registrar General (1859), reprinted by the List and Index Society, Vol 42, 1969 is an essential tool for the family historian, supplemented by the various published guides to the county record offices and other repositories which list not only registers but all the other records they hold on individual chapels. The PRO Class List for RG4 is an updated version of this which eliminates the need to convert a reference in order to select a film. Other listings are to be found in historical and archive journals published often by county or area historical societies, e.g. H Peskett, *Guide to the Parish and Non-Parochial Registers of Devon and Cornwall 1538-1837* (Devon and Cornwall Record Society Series, 1979).

Monthly repository 1806-1832: index & synopsis of the obituaries, compiled by Alan Ruston, Watford, 1985.

Unitarian obituaries 1794-1850, index & synopsis, compiled by Alan Ruston, Watford, 1990.

Obituaries of unitarian ministers 1900-1999, index & synopsis, compiled by Alan Ruston, Supplement to the *Transactions of the Unitarian historical society* April 2000, but obtainable as a separate item.

ENGLISH PRESBYTERIAN, GENERAL BAPTIST AND UNITARIAN CONGREGATIONS IN GREAT BRITAIN LOCATION LIST OF RECORDS

This listing of congregations is by no means complete. Many not recorded here have long disappeared and their records lost. Others have left few extant records and those which remain have little to interest the family historian. This list arose out of a census conducted by the Unitarian Historical Society (UHS) in the 1970s by its secretary, Rev Andrew Hill and gives details of those congregations the whereabouts of whose records have been reported. In its original form it was published in the *Transactions* of the UHS in 1981 and 1982 and the Society has updated it on a master file from subsequent reports from congregations, libraries and record offices.

There are without doubt some errors, both in the listing and with certain items having been deposited in a record office without the UHS being informed. Some records unfortunately may even have been lost since being noted in the 1970s. The situation is of course not static and parts of the list are subject to change, when for example, items are deposited in a repository. As I hope has been made clear in the first section of this guide, there is no central controlling authority within Unitarianism. Each congregation has complete power and responsibility over the disposal of its records and does not have to inform the UHS as to their location. However most congregations have reported on their holdings. The UHS does not have any further information on a congregation's records than is shown in this listing. It is not able to answer genealogical questions as it does not possess a library or data bank.

The congregations are listed in counties for England, and in more general terms for Wales and Scotland, and the county arrangement which existed before 1974 has been used. The record office or similar repository is shown and the records deposited may or may not contain material of use to family historians; each deposit will need to be considered individually. Unfortunately some will contain nothing of genealogical interest whilst others will be a rich source for the researcher. The *List of non-parochial registers and records in the custody of the Registrar General,* published in 1859, reissued 1969 by the List and Index Society, vol. 42 was the key book showing the deposit of these registers, now arranged in the RG 4 series in the Public Record Office. The RG 4 reference has been shown against each holding in the list. The information given here should be sufficient to trace a particular deposit. The International Genealogical Index includes births and pre-1754 marriages extracted from these registers.

The 1859 publication shows the chapels listed as predominantly Presbyterian or Baptist, and there are only a few designated Unitarian. In the 1840s many still clung to the older name, and Unitarian denominational organisation was evolving. Some are termed 'Presbyterian or Independent', a description which goes back to the early eighteenth-century lack of certainty as to denomination. Others evolved away from English Presbyterianism and became Independent; George's Yard, Hammersmith (Middlesex 11 or RG 4/375, 2203, 3595) is in this category, and there are others. It has not been included here as for most of its history this chapel can be considered as part of Independency. Therefore this present listing should be read, at least for the period up to about the 1830s, in conjunction with that contained in *My ancestors were Congregationalists,* compiled by D J H Clifford (Society of Genealogists, first published 1992).

Some chapels were always considered Presbyterian but disappeared before they could be termed Unitarian, or were absorbed into other congregations; the Enfield, Middlesex, Baker Street Meeting and the Uxbridge Meeting are probably in this category. The history of Dissenting churches in London is especially complex, and the denominational ascription of Presbyterian, Independent or Baptist by the Registrar General to several congregations is difficult to substantiate. The Registrar General must have found the classification of many Dissenting chapels problematical to say the least especially as there was another category of chapel found chiefly in Durham and Northumberland labelled 'United Presbyterian' or 'Scotch Church'. Formed after 1800 these were Scottish in origin and organisation and not in the English Presbyterian tradition. They are not listed here. The records of Universalist Churches, of which there were never many, have been included. References to material is almost wholly to original sources and not to secondary or printed material.

An outline listing of the remaining records of the Non-Subscribing Presbyterian Church of Ireland, held in the Public Record Office in Northern Ireland, has been included. This is because this small group of some thirty churches has traditionally been associated with the Unitarian movement in other parts of the UK. Theological disputes in the eighteenth and nineteenth centuries created small synods of churches which eventually formed themselves into the Non-Subscribing Presbyterian Church of Ireland in 1910. Based on the Presbyterian system of church government, the organisation is entirely separate from the Unitarian movement in England, Scotland and Wales.

For those records held by a congregation still in existence contact should be made with the Church Secretary, whose name and address is shown in the *Annual Directory of the General Assembly of Unitarian and Free Christian Churches,* a copy of which is held by many public libraries. In cases of difficulty a copy can be obtained from the General

Assembly at Essex Hall, 1-6 Essex Street, London, WC2R 3HY. Queries or questions relating to family history should not be directed to Essex Hall whose staff are not in a position to respond to them. Please remember that church secretaries may have little interest in genealogical enquiries and there is no requirement that they need to answer a query, certainly if requested over the telephone. When writing always enclose a stamped addressed envelope and if help is given please write back a letter of acknowledgement and thanks.

Abbreviations

- 1932	Date of a congregation's closure;
B	Burial
C	Christening and Baptism
CH	In the possession of the congregation
CL	Central Library
DM	Domestic Mission (a type of chapel opened in deprived city areas in the nineteenth century aimed at assisting the poor)
DW	Dr Williams's Library, 14 Gordon Square, London WC1H OAG
FI	Approximate date of existence
GB	Congregations of General Baptist origin. Most other congregations with origins in the seventeenth and eighteenth centuries may be identified as Presbyterian except when shown otherwise.
GM	Great Meeting
L	Library
M	Meeting
Ma	Marriage
MCL	Manchester Central Library, chiefly Local Studies Library (MFPR refers to microfilm or fiche. Some holdings contain later material than at the PRO)
MH	Meeting House
MI	Monumental Inscription
MS	Manuscript
MSS	Manuscripts
NLW	National Library of Wales, Aberystwyth, Dyfed SY23 3BU
NM	New Meeting
NS	Non-Subscribing
OM	Old Meeting
PL	Public Library
PRO	Public Record Office, Family Records Centre and Kew
RL	Reference Library
RO	Record Office
U	Unitarian
UC	Unitarian College Collection, John Rylands University Library of Manchester, Deansgate, Manchester M3 3EH

CONGREGATIONS IN ENGLAND

BEDFORDSHIRE

BEDFORD
Founded 1960-1990

Location of records not known

LUTON
Founded 1909 meeting in hired rooms
Ceased circa 1920,

NLW (MS 13611B)
Harris Manchester College, Oxford
(Weight Mathews papers)

BERKSHIRE

ABINGDON
Presbyterian

PRO (RG 4/2249) C 1723-1740

NEWBURY
Founded 1662
Built Waterside or Upper Chapel Toomers Ct,
Northbrook St, 1697-1946

DW (38.66; 38.89-94)
PRO (RG 4/269) C 1763-1837,
B 1835-1837

READING
Founded 1876
Built London Rd 1877-1973

contact Mr D O'Rourke, 38 Stanhope St,
Reading, Berks

CAMBRIDGESHIRE

CAMBRIDGE
Founded 1904
Built Memorial Church Emmanuel Rd, 1928

CH; UC (A (1) 11) 2 MS articles

WISBECH
Founded 1784
Built Dead Man's Lane, ?-1898
St Peters, Church Lane. *Unitarian/Baptist*

DW (38.62)
PRO (RG 4/3362) C and B 1783-1837

CHESHIRE

ALLOSTOCK
Founded 1672
Built 1690. *Unitarian*

PRO (RG 4/2259) C and B 1758-1823 *see also* Knutsford Brook St Chapel records RG 8/4, C 1688-1755, Ma 1690-1701, B 1690-1755

ALTRINCHAM
Founded and built Shaw's Lane 1814, Dunham Rd 1872

CH; PRO RG 4/166, *see* Hale Barns

BIRKENHEAD
Founded and built Charing Cross, Grange Rd, 1851 Bessborough Rd, 1903 Clive Rd 1960-76

Cheshire RO (EUC 4); UC (B (1) 42) *see* West Kirby Church records

CHESTER
Founded 1662
Built Crooks Lane, later called Matthew Henry's Chapel 1700, Blacon 1956
Unitarian

Chester City RO (D/MH); DW(38.55); PRO (RG 4/3755, 161, 2090) C 1713-1837, 1848-57, B 1791-1855
H D Roberts, *Matthew Henry and his chapel* (Chester, 1901), contains a list of subscribers (1700)

CONGLETON
Founded 1662. Mill Street
Built Cross St 1687, 1883-1969

Cheshire RO (EUC 8) 1873-1977; PRO (RG 4/211) C 1814-33
Tameside Local Studies L (NU1/23,72)

CREWE
Founded 1862
Built Beech St, 1865-1979

Cheshire RO (EUC 6), Tameside Local Studies L (NU1/36,39)

DEAN ROW
Founded 1672
Built 1694

CH; Cheshire RO (EUC 1; EUC 2/I); MCL (MFPR 340) C 1791-1961, M 1840-1950, B 1827-1969

DUKINFIELD
Stockport. Founded 1678
Built 1708 Old Chapel 1840

Tameside RO (NU1/61; NU/2 1-72);
PRO (RG 4/165, 576, 1799, 2520,
3764A), C 1676-1713 and 1762-1840,
Ma 1676-1713, B1676-1713, 1761-93,
1837-38. MCL (MFPR 294).
A Gordon, *History* (Manchester, 1896)
gives selected MIs.

HALE BARNS
Founded 1662
Built 1723

CH; UC (D4)
PRO (RG 4/166), C 1733-1836, *see*
Altrincham

HYDE
Flowery Field
Founded and built Newton St 1831, 1878

CH

HYDE
Gee Cross, Stockport
Founded & built Hyde Chapel, Stockport Rd
1708, 1848

CH; PRO (RG 4/98, 99, 171, 548, 549,
2262), C 1710-1838, B 1785-1826,
MCL (MFPR 296); Tameside Local
Studies L (NU1/ 58; NU4; DD 237 V)

KNUTSFORD, NETHER
Founded 1672. The Old Dissenting Chapel
Built Brook St 1689

CH; PRO (RG 4/190), C and B
1792-1836

MACCLESFIELD
Founded 1672
Built King Edward St 1690

Cheshire RO (EUC 3); PRO (RG 4/216,
2904, 3535), C 1713-1837

MACCLESFIELD
Founded Parsonage St, 1847-84

Cheshire RO (EUC 3/18/23/1-2) PRO
(RG 4/216,2904,3535) C 1713-1837

NANTWICH
Founded 1672
Built Hospital St 1686, 1726-1963

Cheshire RO (EUC 7/1-10) PRO
(RG 4/168), C 1783-94, 1811-1835,
B 1821-35; Tameside Local Studies
L (NU1/24, 63-4)

NANTWICH
Founded circa 1813. Unitarian Baptist PRO (RG4/189, C 1781-1835)
Barker St, joined Baptist New Connexion 1862

NORTHWICH
Founded early nineteenth century Tameside Local Studies L (NU1/22)

SALE
Founded 1699. Manchester CL Archives Dept
Built 1715, Cross St 1739, Atkinson Rd (M210 B, M & C 1924-1965)
1876-1970

STOCKPORT
Founded 1681 Stockport PL; PRO (RG 4/198, 419,
Built 1702 High St ,1722 St Petersgate, 1800, 1801) C 1761-1780, 1792-1798,
1842 Cheadle, 1973 1826-1837, B 1761-1780
Tameside Local Studies L (NU11/60)

STOCKPORT
New Chapel, Hillgate PRO (RG 4/197, 199), C 1785-1828,
B 1785-1837

STYAL
Founded and built 1824, Norcliffe Cheshire RO (EUC 2 CH);
Chapel 1867, Pownall Fee, Wilmslow PRO (RG 4/1104), C 1833-36 also at
Quarry Bank Chapel MCL (MFPR 295).

WEST KIRBY
Founded 1906. Cheshire RO (EUC 5)
Built 1910, Brookfield Gdns ,1928

CORNWALL

FALMOUTH and FLUSHING
Founded 1812-54 Cornwall RO (little original material)

CUMBERLAND

CARLISLE
Founded 1883.
Built Victoria Viaduct 1889,
Lorne St 1939-57

Cumbria RO (CAE 1/82; 4/1988;
4/2002); Leeds Mill Hill Chapel
(87); DW

PENRITH
Rowcliffe Lane

PRO (RG 4/4458), C 1789-1837

WORKINGTON
Presbyterian

PRO (RG 4/65,1881, 2025,2267)
C 1745-1837

DERBYSHIRE

ASHFORD-IN-THE-WATER
Founded 1696-1875.
Built about 1700 Cliff End

see local parish records.
Graveyard survives

BELPER
Founded 1689
Built Field Row 1716, 1788

CH

BRADWELL
Founded and Built 1695-1954, Old Chapel

UC (D4)

BUXTON
Founded 1672
Built 1690 Hartington Rd 1711-1967

Derbyshire RO; Tameside Local Studies
L (NU1/21, 25 and 74); UC (unlisted)

CHESTERFIELD
Founded 1662
Built Elder Yard 1694

CH; Chesterfield PL (ELD 1-71)
DW (94K11 Odgers)
PRO (RG 4/73, 516) C 1708-1837, B
1705-1837); Shrewsbury PL (Astley
papers); UC (A(1) 14) Register of
Goodwyn Barmby

DERBY
Founded 1672
Built Friargate 1698

CH; Derbyshire RO
PRO (RG 4/5, 499, 2033, 2034), C 1698-1836, B 1714, 1796-1836; UC unlisted

DUFFIELD
Founded and built 1766-1867

PRO (RG 4/501, 2268) C 1750-73, 1806-35

FINDERN
Founded 1690. Built ?-1866. OM

PRO (RG 4/502), C 1785-94

FLAGG
Founded and built 1839-1963

Sheffield CL (VCR 1997. 1-2); *see* Manchester Unitarian District Association records; UC (unlisted). This building is now an Anglican church but still owned and occasionally used by Unitarians

GLOSSOP
Founded 1871. Built 1875 Fitzalan St 1896

CH; Glossop Heritage Society: UC

GREAT HUCKLOW
Founded and built 1696, 1795

CH, PRO (RG 4/49), C 1789-1826; MCL (MFPR 301)

ILKESTON
Founded 1700. OM
Built High St 1719, 1869-1930

PRO (RG 4/3523), C 1735-1820

NORTON
Founded 1690
Built 1794-1843

PRO (RG 4/508), C 1777-1836

STONEY MIDDLETON
Founded 1846. Closed about 1850

Sheffield CL (UCR 61. 1-9)

DEVON

BOW
Founded 1753-1816

Devon RO (2011 D)

COLYTON
Founded 1662
Built OM or George's M 1745-1939
MS history 1911 among Exeter
Assembly records
Unitarian

Somerset RO (D/N/ tau. mst 6/6
D/N/wu 1/8 & 2/10)
PRO (RG 4/2276), C 1773-1836, C and
B 1832-36, RG8/6, C 1824-1862.
B 1832-1862. UC (unlisted).

CREDITON
Founded 1672
Built Bell Court, Bowden Hill 1721-1965

Devon RO (2011d); DW (94K13
Odgers)
PRO (RG 4/4, 843, 3558) C 1735-
1837, B 1828-37

CULLOMPTON
Founded 1662
Built Pound Square 1698, 1913

CH; PRO (RG 4/13, 2097, 519),
C 1693-1823, C and B 1823-37
Devon RO

DARTMOUTH
Presbyterian

PRO (RG 4/0959), C 1726-1837

DEVONPORT
Founded 1790
Built George St 1791, Granby St 1829,
Christ Church, Duke St 1864-1917. *Unitarian*

PRO (RG 4/524), C 1828-35

EXETER
Bow Meeting

PRO (RG 4/965), C & B 1687-1823,
see Exeter George's Meeting

EXETER
Founded 1662
Built James' M 1687, George's M, South St
1760-1984

Devon RO (71/18)
DW (38. 53-4; 38.58 94K17 Odgers)
PRO (RG 4/47, 1085), C and B 1824-1837, B 1818-1822

EXETER
Founded and built 1719-1810, Mint M
united with George's M

PRO (RG 4/336), C 1719-1810 *see*
Exeter George's Meeting

GULLIFORD
Founded 1662
Built Gulliford, Woodbury 1689, 1774
Lympstone 1820-before 1900; Exeter,
George's M

Devon RO (2861 D/R1) Topsham
register with Gulliford entries; PRO
(RG 4/1226), C 1773-1837, B 1786-1835)

HONITON
GB Founded 1737, Bridge MH High St –
1860; Baptist/Presbyterian

PRO (RG 4/2027). Births 1829-1837

MORETON HAMPSTEAD
Founded 1662
Built Cross Chapel 1692, 1802

UC (C(2)6)
PRO (RG 4/444), C 1672-1836

MORETON HAMPSTEAD
GB Founded 1690
Built Fore St 1786-1818, united with Cross
Chapel *see* Cross St Chapel Records

OTTERY St MARY
Presbyterian

PRO (RG4/2029), C 1746-1785,
B 1746-1837

PLYMOUTH

Founded 1662
Built Treville St; Norley St 1823,
Notte St 1958. *Unitarian*

CH; Plymouth Corporation hold deeds
of Treville St.
PRO (RG 4/2159, 2537, 4091), C 1672-
1835, B 1662-1695.
Other records destroyed in blitz.

PLYMOUTH

Batter Street

PRO (RG 4/1091, 1217, 1218),
C 1704-1837, B 1768-1837

SIDMOUTH

Founded and built Upper High St 1710
Higher meeting

CH; PRO (RG 4/1219), C 1753-1836
B 1831-1834

TAVISTOCK

Founded 1660, Abbey Chapel Bedford Sq,
1660-1959

Devon RO (1154D)
PRO (RG 4/2030), C 1692-1837,

TOPSHAM

Founded before 1687
Built 1723-27, 1890

Devon RO (2861D); Somerset RO
(D/N/wu 4); UC (A (1)14, D7, D11)
PRO (RG 4/1222), C 1744-1837, B
1771-1837; *see* Cullompton Chapel
records

TORQUAY

Founded 1883
Built Montpelier Rd 1912

CH

DORSET

BOURNEMOUTH

Founded 1882
Built West Hill Rd 1891, Hinton Rd 1991

CH; Dorset RO

BRIDPORT
Founded and built East St 1672, 1794

Dorset RO (N1; Colfox family papers D43/R1-7) PRO (RG 4/344, 2160, 2406, 2407), C 1720-1837, B 1820-35

DORCHESTER
Founded 1662
Built Pease Lane 1720- c.1840

Dorset RO (D43; R8 Colfox family records)
Somerset RO (D/N/wu 4)
PRO (RG 4/345, 459), C 1750-1836

POOLE
Founded 1690
Built 1705 Hill St OM 1868-1968

Dorset RO (N3/1-24);
PRO (RG 4/464), C 1750-1837, B 1766-1836.

WAREHAM
Founded 1828
Built South St 1830-1976

PRO (RG 4/1727), C 1788-1837

WEYMOUTH
Founded 1892-96

Dorset RO (N. U. 3/I)

DURHAM

BISHOP WEARMOUTH
Smyrna Chapel

PRO (RG 4/3435), C 1797-1837

DARLINGTON
Founded 1852
Built Lead Yd 1873-1922
see Stockton Chapel records

GATESHEAD
Half-Moon Lane Chapel

PRO (RG 4/1765), C 1783-1837

SOUTH SHIELDS
Formerly Low MH

RG8/11, C 1786-1857, Ma 1845-1850, B 1847-1851

STOCKTON ON TEES
Founded 1688. OM
Built High St 1699, Wellington St 1873

CH; Northumberland RO (ZAN M
17/16)
PRO (RG4/481, 1097), C 1688-1836,
Ma 1688-1709, Deaths 1690-1774

SUNDERLAND
Spring Garden Lane Chapel

PRO (RG 4/484, 595) C 1766-1837

SUNDERLAND
Founded 1814
Built Bridge Square 1831-1967
Bishopwearmouth. *Unitarian*

Tyne and Wear Archive Services (with
Newcastle Divine Unity Church
records); PRO (RG 4/3421), C 1823-1837

WICKHAM
Ebenezer Chapel, Swalwell

PRO (RG 4/591, 1237), C 1733-1836

ESSEX

COLCHESTER
Founded 1672
Built Helen's Lane MH c.1692-1823
later Stockwell Chapel

Suffolk RO, Ipswich (FG 4/1/15/89
and 93);
PRO (RG 4/2907), C 1784-1815,
1814-1837

ILFORD
Founded 1906
Built High Rd 1909-79

DW

LEYTONSTONE
Founded 1912
Built Knotty Green, Lea Bridge Rd 1931-60

DW

SAFFRON WALDEN
GB. Founded 1711
Built Hill St 1792, joined Baptist Union 1915

PRO (RG 4/783, 784, 785, 786, 2285),
C 1790-1824,1826-37, B 1791-1820

SOUTHEND-ON-SEA
Founded 1897
Built Darnley Rd 1898, Grange Gds 1977

CH, Essex RO, Southend (D/NZ. 13)

WALTHAMSTOW
Built 1730. Marsh St, OM House
ceased circa 1840

PRO (RG 4/779), C 1796-1825 UC (D4)

WALTHAMSTOW
Founded 1895
Built 1897-1940 Truro Rd

DW

GLOUCESTERSHIRE

CHELTENHAM
Founded 1832
Built Bayshill 1844

CH

CIRENCESTER
Founded and built Gosditch St 1672-1969

DW (2 boxes; 38.88)

FRENCHAY
Winterbourne
Founded and built 1691

CH; PRO (RG 4/622), C 1814-37,
B 1806-37

GLOUCESTER
Founded 1662
Built Barton St 1699-1967, now meets
Friends MH

Somerset RO (D/N/wu4)
Shrewsbury PL (Astley papers 1067)
PRO (2164, 2165, 3566), C 1740-1836
B 1785-1836

MARSHFIELD
Founded 1680
Built 1699, 1752-1883

Bath RO *see* Bath Trim St Chapel
records

STROUD
Founded 1876-91 Lansdowne Rd

Somerset RO (D/n/wu)

THORNBURY
Presbyterian/Independent

PRO (RG 4/711), C 1796-1837,
B 1816-1836

WOOTTON UNDER EDGE
Old Town MH

PRO (RG 4/712), C 1767-1837

HAMPSHIRE AND ISLE OF WIGHT

NEWPORT
GB Founded 1726
Built Pyle St, 1728 High St 1774

Isle of Wight RO (NC/U); UC (D11);
PRO (RG 4/36, 42), C 1739-1837

PORTSMOUTH
Founded 1662
Built Penny St 1691, High St 1718, John
Pounds Memorial Church 1956

Portsmouth RO (257A)
PRO (RG 4/405, 406, 564), C 1676-
1857, B 1787-1853

PORTSMOUTH
John Pounds DM nineteenth century

Portsmouth RO (257A/1/11/4)

PORTSMOUTH
GB Founded 1640
Built St Thomas St 1693, 1715, 1865-1946
united with High Street

Portsmouth RO (257A/1/12)
UC (C(1) 11)
PRO (RG 4/2304), C and B 1785-1837

RINGWOOD
Founded 1672
Built St Thomas Chapel, M H Lane 1727-1975

PRO (RG 4/655), C 1748-1837,
B 1815-37

RYDE
Founded about 1876-1900

Portsmouth RO (257/A/1/6/1)

SOUTHAMPTON
Founded 1847
Built Church of the Saviour London Rd
1860, 1956

CH; Southampton RO (D/I.Y/24/1-10)
Edmund Kell papers; UC (C(1) 11)

HEREFORDSHIRE

HERTFORDSHIRE

CHESHUNT
Founded 1705. Crossbrook Street

PRO (RG 4/1377), C 1729-99

ST ALBANS
Founded 1662
Built Lower Dagnall Lane 1697-1893

Hertfordshire RO (D/EOY T11); DW;
PRO (RG 4/749), C 1751-1836

LETCHWORTH
Founded 1925. Howard Hall-1958

Hertfordshire RO (NU1/1-7)

WARE
OM House, Swan Yard

PRO (RG 4/672), C 1787-1807

WATFORD
U Fellowship. Founded 1947 meeting at
the Friends MH

CH

HUNTINGDONSHIRE

YAXLEY
Presbyterian

PRO (RG 4/1109), C 1820-1837

KENT

BIDDENDEN
GB Founded 1648.
Built 1834-68

UC (D62) 1828-34

CANTERBURY
GB Founded 1642, occupied thirteenth
century Blackfriars 1732-1913

UC (D62); DW (38. 78, 38. 81)
PRO (RG/751), Births 1780-1836,
B 1785-1836; *see also* E Kent, E & W
Kent GB churches; Kent & Sussex U
Christian Association records. Registers
1780-1836 have been transcribed, *see*
General Baptist Assembly Occasional
Paper no 17 (1992)

CHATHAM

GB Founded 1600.

Built Heavyside Lane 1802, Hammond Hill later Church of the Great Companions 1882

CH; PRO (RG 4/755, 756), Births 1700-1837, B 1785-1837; *see also* Kent and Sussex U Christian Association Registers have been transcribed, *see* General Baptist Assembly Occasional Paper no. 13 (1991)

CRANBROOK

GB Founded ?

Built High St 1808-75

UC (D62) DW (OD 329/3)

PRO (RG 4/917), Births 1682-1778, B 1809-37

DEAL

GB Founded 1682

Built High St ?-1830 then closed and opened again until 1910

DW (94K14 Odgers); *see also* E Kent, E and W Kent GB churches; Kent and Sussex U Christian Association records

DEPTFORD

Church Street GB Founded and built 1674, 1802-1967

DW (OD 15-16); PRO (RG 4/4184) B 1824-36

Kent and Sussex U Association records DW (OD 329/2)

DOVER

GB Founded and built, Adrian St 1643, 1745, 1819

CH; DW (38.208); UC (C(2)8); *see also* E Kent and W Kent GB Kent churches, and Sussex U Christian Association records.

DOVER

Presbyterian

PRO (RG 4/1376), C 1710-1776, B 1732-1744

HEADCORN

GB Founded about 1775

Built 1819 joined Baptist Union 1915

UC (D62); PRO (RG 4/932), Births 1731-1837, B 1780-1837; *see also* Kent and Sussex U Christian Association records

MAIDSTONE
Founded 1662
Built Earl St 1736

CH; PRO (RG 4/936), C 1732-1825, 1785-1825

MAIDSTONE and TOVIL
GB nineteenth century

UC (D9; D62)

NORTHIAM
GB Founded 1796. Built Herman Hill 1810

East Sussex RO (NU4/ 1-6)

RAMSGATE
Birchington GB. Founded 1762 closed 1884

DW *see* Kent and Sussex U Christian Association records

ROCHESTER

PRO (RG 8/19) C 1700-1808

ROLVENDEN
GB Founded seventeenth century, 1800-90

DW, UC (D62); PRO (Kent separate MS of Births); CRO; *see also* Kent and Sussex U Christian Association records

SEVENOAKS
Bessels Green, Orpington. Founded 1650, Built OM 1716

CH; Sevenoaks CL; PRO (RG 4/1728), Births 1650-1837, B 1739-1837
UC (D 11)

SMARDEN
GB Bell Meeting. Founded and built about 1741-1845

DW MSS 38-117 (Church Book 1640-1845) Graveyard still survives

TENTERDEN
Founded 1690
Built OM Ashford Rd 1746

CH; UC (D62)
PRO (RG 4/1987),C 1736-1837
B 1812-37
Kent RO (A1352/3)

TUNBRIDGE WELLS
GB Founded 1646-1813

DW (38.71)

WOOLWICH AND PLUMSTEAD
Founded 1894.   DW
Built 1917 Dallin Rd, 1930-45

LANCASHIRE

ACCRINGTON
Founded 1859   Bolton CL (NUL 11/1)
Built Oxford St 1868, 1966

AINSWORTH
Founded 1662. Cockey Moor, Middleton   CH; Lancashire RO (PR 2829/1-7)
Built 1672, 1715   PRO (RG 4/1015, 1195, 2311, 2312)
                                                C 1769-1837, B 1781-1837

ASHTON-IN-MAKERFIELD
Park Lane, Winwick Founded 1672,   Wigan RO, Leigh (D/NUI); UC
Built 1697   B (2)15; C (2) 9).
                                                PRO (RG 4, 886, 1124, 2445) C
                                                1786-1792, 1795-1837, B 1800-1821,
                                                1823-1837

ASHTON UNDER LYNE
Founded 1897   CH
Built 1900 Richmond Hill 1907

ASTLEY
Leigh. Founded 1823-40   PRO (RG 4/18), C 1825-37
Unitarian

ASTLEY
Founded 1856   CH
Built Manchester Rd 1865

ATHERTON
Chowbent, Leigh. Newbent Chapel   Wigan RO; UC (C1)
Founded and built 1645, 1721   PRO (RG 4/48, 1329, 1330), C & B
                                                1758-1837

BLACKPOOL

North Shore. Founded 1873
Built Dickson Rd 1883-1975

Lancashire RO (UBe)
Bolton CL (NUL8)

BLACKPOOL

South Shore. Founded 1894
Built Lytham Rd 1903

CH; Lancashire RO (DDX 207/6 and 112)

BOLTON

Founded 1862. Commission St 1868, Unity
Church, Dean Rd 1893

Bolton CL (NUL 11/1)

BOLTON

Founded and built Halliwell Rd 1899, 1931

CH

BOLTON-LE-MOORS

Founded 1672
Built Bank St 1696

1856 CH; UC (C(1) 11, 54 and unlisted);
PRO (RG 4/64, 2004), ZC 1753-1836;
Bolton CL. G M Ramsden,
A Responsible Society (1985), gives
biographical details of leading families

BOLTON LE-MOORS

Moor Lane. Founded 1822-c.1843
see Bolton Bank St Chapel records

PRO (RG 4/1022), ZC 1793-1836,
B 1813-1815. MCL (MFPR 267)

BOOTLE

Founded 1889
Built Stanley Rd 1895-1972

Records held by solicitor (Alsop,
Stevenson, Bateson of Water Street,
Liverpool); UC B(1) 42 and unlisted.

BURNLEY

Founded 1858
Built Trafalgar Rd 1871-1960

UC (unlisted)

BURY
Founded and built Silver St 1719, Bank St 1974

CH; UC (A (2) 14, A (1) 8 and 9, 1852, C (2) 9, D9)
PRO (RG 4/807, 1203), C 1723-1737, B 1832-1837

BURY
Chesham. Founded and built Halstead St, 1883-1974 united with Bank St 1972

CH

CHORLEY
Founded and built Park St, 1725
Unitarian

Lancashire RO (U Ch)
PRO (RG 4/1031), C 1782-1836

CHORLTON-upon-MEDLOCK
Moseley St. Founded and built 1789
Presbyterian and Unitarian

Manchester CL Archives dept (M30/I-5)

CHORLTON-upon-MEDLOCK
Upper Brook St, 1839-1921

PRO (RG 4/131, 2856) C 1787-1837, 1840-55; UC (unlisted).

COLNE
Founded 1876
Built Stanley St 1879, Byrom Rd 1970-79

Lancashire RO (Accs 4454, 5110)

CROFT
Founded and built Lady Lane, 1839-195

Wigan RO with Atherton, Chowbent records

DARWEN
Founded 1877
Built Bolton St 1879-93

Bolton CL (NUL9)

DENTON
Founded 1875
Built Wilton St 1879

CH

ECCLES
Monton Green. Founded 1662
Built 1698, 1802 Monton Church 1875

Lancashire RO
PRO (RG 4/1035, 1036), C 1785-1837, B 1801-37. Salford Archives Centre (N/UNI); MCL (MFPR 20)

EGERTON
Walmsley. Turton Founded 1671
Built 1713

CH; PRO (RG 4/1622), C 1762-1836, B 1786-1837

HEATON MOOR
Founded 1893-1910

UC (C(2)1)

HEYWOOD
Founded 1856
Built Brittain Hill 1860-1910

Bolton Central Library NUL (11/1);
Lancashire RO (0L11 5XT)

HINDLEY
Wigan. Founded and built 1641,
Market St, 1700

CH; DW (94K21)
PRO (RG 4/823 2115, 2316), C 1644-1836, Ma 1644-77, B 1642-1754

HORWICH
Founded 1890
Built Church St 1896

CH; DW (95.22 Odgers)

LANCASTER
Founded 1687
Built St Nicholas St 1726, 1786,
Scotforth Rd 1966

CH; PRO (RG 4/2117), C & B 1771-1836, UC (A(1) 14).
MCL may contain some material in MFPR 272.

LEIGH
Founded 1887. Built Twist Lane 1897

CH

LEIGH
Chowbent, Newbent Chapel
see Atherton

LIVERPOOL
Bold St, Universalist Chapel
Founded 1825-?

PRO (RG 4/1483), C 1825-37

LIVERPOOL
Dingle. Founded and built Toxteth Park
1618, 1714

CH; UC (B(1) 42)
PRO (RG 4/1054),C 1778-1855
also at MCL MFPR 274 B 1785-1855
Liverpool RO (288 HAL 3/1-7)

LIVERPOOL
Everton. Founded and built North End
DM Bond St, 1859-1909 amalgamated with
Roscommon St Chapel 1862 and Hamilton
Rd DM 1896-1974

Liverpool RO (266 NOR, 2B8ULL/9/3)

LIVERPOOL
Garston. Founded 1899
Built 1910-20

Records held by solicitor (Alsop, Stevenson, Bateson of Water Street, Liverpool)

LIVERPOOL
Gateacre, Childwall. Founded 1690
Built Gateacre Brow 1700

CH; DW (94K18 Odgers); UC (D58);
PRO (RG 4/821), C 1711-1836

LIVERPOOL
Kaye St. Founded 1693
Built 1707, Paradise St Chapel 1791,
Hope St 1848-1962 YMCA Mt Pleasant
1962-79

Liverpool RO (288H0P; 28BULL/8/4;
288ULL/9/l; 900 MD; 288HA/ 5/6)
Tameside Local Studies L (NU1/50-53);
DW (95.26 Odgers) UC (D12, B (1)
42 and unlisted)
PRO (RG 4/972, 1043, 1044), C 1709-
1837 and at MCL (MFPR 273 C 1709-
1837)
H D Roberts, *Hope St Church* (1909),
gives biographical detail

LIVERPOOL
Founded 1762
Built Octagon Chapel, Temple Court 1763-76
Unitarian

Liverpool RO (288ULL/8/1/2);
PRO (RG 4/3126) C 1762-80

LIVERPOOL
St Thomas St. Founded 1822-?

UC (D 12), Liverpool RO (288 HAL/15)

LIVERPOOL
Sefton Park. Founded and built Castle Hey
1688, Benn's Gdns 1727, Renshaw St
1811, Ullet Rd 1899

CH; Liverpool RO (288ULL; 900 MDI);
Dyfed RO (Acc 5132); UC (B (1) 42);
PRO (RG 4/1042, 1481, 1482, 2170,
2171) C 1719-1837, B 1819-37 and at
MCL (MFPR 273). There is a published
transcription of the Renshaw St Church
Burying Ground by Marples & Co., 1903

LIVERPOOL
Toxteth Park. Founded Liverpool DM
Society 1836
Built Bedford St 1854, Mill St 1892-1978,
Wellington Rd School (mission) 1978

Ancient Chapel of Toxteth records;
Liverpool RO (266DOM): UC B (1) 42.

LYTHAM ST ANNES
Founded 1905
Built 1906 Channing Rd, Ansdell 1930

CH; Lancashire RO (DBX 207/119)

MANCHESTER
Blackley. Founded 1689
Built 1697, 1884-1966
Presbyterian and Unitarian

DW (94K6); PRO (RG 4/1460) C and B
1756-1837: MCL (MFPR 267); UC
(unlisted)

MANCHESTER
Chorlton cum Hardy. Founded 1890
Built Wilbraham Rd 1900

CH

MANCHESTER

Cross St. Founded 1662

Built Cross St 1694, 1959

CH; Manchester CL Archives Dept (MS027.842M10; MS274.273M37; MSf285.2P8; MS922.81G1; MSf929. 5M28; M22/1/3/7; MISC/170) John Rylands Univ L (Lancashire 1st classis minutes etc; poor book); UC (A (1) 13 and unlisted; D4) PRO (RG 4/63, 976, 2009, 2010, 2857) C 1712-1838, B 1785-87 and 1791-1840). MCL (MFPR 277)

MANCHESTER

Failsworth. Founded 1688

Built Dob Lane 1698, 1879

CH; PRO (RG 4/2788), C 1803-36, MCL (L 71) C 1691-1807. A Gordon, *History* (Manchester, 1904), contains a transcription of the registers 1701-1836

MANCHESTER

Gorton. Founded 1694

Built 1703, Brookfield Church 1871

CH; MCL (MFPR 182), C 1732-1881, M 1864-81, B 1785-81; M 74/16 (archives) has a transcription of the grave plan.

MANCHESTER

Longsight. Founded 1866

Built Birch Lane 1883-1950

Manchester District Association records

MANCHESTER

Moss Side. Founded 1887

Built Shrewsbury St 1892, 1901-47

UC (Cupboard C)

MANCHESTER

Rusholme. Founded 1672

Built Platt Chapel 1700, 1791-1973

Manchester CL Archives Dept M 59 (MF); MCL (MFPR 189) C 1687-1807, M 1865-1973, B 1786-1918, 1946-53)

MANCHESTER
Hulme. Founded 1859
Built DM Renshaw St 1868-1976

Records held by solicitor (Tatham Worthington of Manchester)

MANCHESTER
Strangeways. Founded and built Bridge St 1838, Broughton 1903-13

Manchester CL Archives Dept M 43 C 1881-1905, M 1840-1903; UC (1) 42

MANCHESTER
Wythenshawe. Founded 1935

Manchester Unitarian District Association. Built Brownlow Rd 1936, 1959-76 records

MIDDLETON
Founded 1860
Old Road. Built 1893-1965

see Manchester Unitarian District Association records

MOSSLEY
Founded 1841
Built Stamford Rd 1852

CH; Tameside Local Studies L (NU1/26, 59); UC (unlisted Fox mss)

MOTTRAM
Founded 1841
Built Hyde Rd, 1846

CH

NELSON
Founded 1904
Built Eleanor St, 1912-31

Bolton CL (NUL10)

NEWCHURCH
Forest of Rossendale. Founded 1806
Built 1809, Bethlehem U Chapel 1865

CH; PRO (RG 4/1332) C 1807-38; MCL (MFPR 285)

OLDHAM
Founded 1813
Built Lord St 1816, 1877, King St 1971

CH; Oldham Archives Centre (Misc 59); UC (unlisted)

ORMSKIRK
Founded 1662
Chapel St 1696, Aughton St 1783-1886

PRO (RG 4/3584), C 1743-1837; Built (MFPR 280) MCL

PADIHAM
Whaley. Founded 1806
Built 1823, Knight Hill 1874
Unitarian

CH; PRO (RG 4/1058, 1059, 3893)
C 1823-37, B 1830-37
Lancashire RO (DDX 462.80-85)

PILKINGTON
Stand Lane

PRO (RG 4/1147, 2318) C 1765-1837

PRESCOT
Founded and built Atherton St, 1757-c.1879

PRO (RG 4/1120), C 1776-1837,
B 1786-1836

PRESTON
Founded 1672
Built 1716-1975 Church Street
now meets elsewhere
Unitarian

CH; Lancashire RO (U Pr)
Shrewsbury PL (Astley papers 1067)
PRO (RG 4/1149, 1150) C 1763-1817,
1763-1837, B 1783-1836

RAWTENSTALL
Founded and built 1757, Bank St 1853, 1971

CH

RIVINGTON
Bolton. Founded 1662
Built 1703

CH; Bolton Archives (register)
PRO (RG 4/989) C 1784-1819, B 1789-
1850. Registers and MIs transcribed
and printed by Holding and Rogers,
1988 *see* Bolton Bank St Chapel
records.

ROCHDALE
Founded 1662
Built Lower Gates 1672, Blackwater St 1717,
1857 Clover St 1974; (Founded and built
Providence Chapel 1818 combined with
Clover St 1890)

CH; DW (95.38)
PRO (RG 4/990), C 1785-1837, B
1802-37 also at MCL MFPR 284;
Shrewsbury PL (Astley papers) Bolton
CL (NUL 11/1)

ROCHDALE
Spotland, Hallfold Chapel

PRO (RG 4/2042, 2043, 2044, 2176,
2910, 3186) C 1752-1821, B 1790-
1794, 1826-1837)

ST HELENS
Founded 1901
Built Corporation St 1904, 1950

CH

SALFORD
Founded and built 1825, Green Gate
mid-nineteenth century
Unitarian

PRO (RG 4/1616, 1617) C 1825-37,
B 1826-37

SALFORD
Pendleton. Founded 1861
Built Cross Lane 1874, 1976

CH

SOUTHPORT
Founded 1862
Built Portland St 1867

CH; UC B (1) 42

STALYBRIDGE
Founded 1865
Built Canal St 1870

CH

SWINTON
Founded 1820
Built 1831, Swinton Hall Rd 1857-1983;
Unitarian

Salford Archives Centre (N/UN2);
PRO (RG 4/1291) B 1833-1837

THORNTON CLEVELEYS
U Fellowship. Founded 1963-82

Lancashire RO (U. Th)

TOTTINGTON
Lower End, Dundee Chapel

PRO (RG 4/1621) C 1699-1730,
1800-1837

TURTON
Walmsley Chapel. Founded 1671
Built 1713

PRO (RG 4/1622) C 1762-1836,
B 1786-1837

URMSTON
Founded 1894
Built Queens Rd, 1900

CH

WALLASEY
Founded 1888
Built Iron Church Manor Rd, 1892
Memorial Church Manor Rd 1899

CH; UC B (1) 42.

WARRINGTON
Founded 1662
Sankey Street Chapel
Built 1703 Cairo Street, 1745

CH; DW (Odgers papers);
PRO (RG 4/1623), C 1724-1837.
B 1786-1837
MCL (929.34 2719Wal) C 1724-1853,
B 1788-1960. UC (B(1)42).
The registers and MIs have been
transcribed and printed (J K Bulmer,
1980) 1749-1969.

WHITEFIELD
Stand Lane, Pilkington. Founded 1672
Built 1693, 1819, 1955

CH; Manchester CL Archives Dept (L31)
PRO (RG 4/1147, 2318) C 1765-1837,
B 1823-37 also at MCL (MFPR 281)

LEICESTERSHIRE

ASHBY-DE-LA-ZOUCHE
Barden Park

PRO (RG 4/1173) C 1756-1837

COALVILLE
Founded 1905
Built Bridge Street, 1908-46

Leicestershire RO (NN/73/1-11)

HINCKLEY
Founded 1672
Built GM Baines Lane, 1722

CH; DW (94K20); UC (C (1) 11)
PRO (RG 4/1438, 1626, 3894)
C 1706-1837, B 1787-1794, 1813-37

LEICESTER

Founded 1662

Built GM East Bond St, 1708

CH; DW (95.25 Odgers)
PRO (RG 4/1299, 1627, 1628, 2323, 2324, 3189) C I711-40, 1743-1838, B 1773-1837, Leicestershire RO (NN/179/28-217)

LEICESTER

Founded 1845. Domestic Mission
(Part of Great Meeting)

Leicestershire RO (NN/179)

LEICESTER

Founded 1866

Built Wellington St,

later Narborough Rd 1875-1979

Leicestershire RO (N/IJ/179)

LOUGHBOROUGH

Founded 1672

Built 1744, Victoria Rd 1864

Presbyterian & Unitarian

DW (95.28)
PRO (RG 4/78) C 1791-1836, Deaths 1824-1825; Leicestershire RO (NN/207/1-125)

MOUNT SORRELL

Founded and built about 1700-1846

Unitarian

PRO (RG 4/78) C 1791-1836, Deaths 1824-1825 Leicestershire RO (N/U/207/93.4)

NARBOROUGH

Presbyterian

PRO (RG 4/2912) C 1755-1790. Deaths 1756-1785

LINCOLNSHIRE

BOSTON

Founded and built Spain Lane 1804, 1819

Unitarian

CH; PRO (RG 4/3131), B 1820-37; PRO (RG 37/17)

1864.

TERMS AND REGULATIONS

OF THE

NEW GRAVEL-PIT BURIAL-GROUND,

ATTACHED TO THE

UNITARIAN CHURCH, HACKNEY.

TERMS.

	To Congregation.	To Non-subscribers.
Ground for a Double Vault or Brick Grave for 12 Coffins,		
9 ft. by 6½ ft. £20 0 0		— £24 0 0
Ditto for a Single Vault or Brick Grave for 6 Coffins,		
9 ft. by 4 ft. 15 0 0		— 18 0 0
Additional Ground, 5s. per square foot.		
Family Earth Grave, 11 ft. deep, for 3 Coffins 6 0 0		— 7 4 0
Interment of a single Corpse 2 0 0		— 2 8 0
Ditto of a Child under 10 years of age 1 0 0		— 1 4 0

The Expenses of construction of Vaults and digging Graves to be paid by the Purchasers,
who are to remove all rubbish and restore the Ground to its original state.

Fee for Opening and Re-closing a Double Vault £1 5 0
Ditto   ditto   a Single Vault 0 15 0
For Opening and Filling-up a Family Earth Grave 0 15 0

The above Charges do not include the Fee to the officiating Minister.

REGULATIONS.

To the Poor Members of the Congregation half the above Charges will be remitted.

The Undertaker is to give in the name, age, day of death and late abode of the Deceased, *in writing*, before the interment takes place, for the purpose of registration.

Certificated copies of the Register may be obtained by application to the Minister, on payment to him of Half-a-crown.

Grave-stones must be put up within Six Months after the interment, or the right will be forfeited. Copies of Inscriptions must be shewn to the Minister or Treasurer before they are inscribed on the Tomb-stones.

Applications concerning Funerals to be made to the Minister or Treasurer, through the Sexton, who resides in the Dwelling-house in the Burial-ground.

This is not untypical of prospectuses issued by 19th Century chapels. Hackney was probably more expensive than most. The church has disappeared but the burial ground remains.

GAINSBOROUGH
Founded 1672
Built Trinity St; Beaumont St 1721,
1928-74; North Midland U Assoc.
Presbyterian & Unitarian

PRO (RG 4/25A, 2454, 2455, 2456,
4061A) C 1707-1836

KIRKSTEAD
Woodall. Founded 1715
Built 1721

Lincolnshire RO (TLE 32/11-15)
PRO (RG 4/1756) C 1822-36

LINCOLN
Founded 1662
Built High St, 1725

CH; DW (38.63); GB

LONG SUTTON (LUTTON)
Founded 1700, joined Baptist Union 1915

DW (38.76); UC (D6)

STAMFORD
Founded 1756, date of closure unknown

DW (95.41-2 Odgers)

LONDON
BERMONDSEY
Founded 1882
Built Fort Rd 1888-1940

DW

BETHNAL GREEN
DM. Founded 1832
Built Spicer St 1836, Mansford St 1889

CH

BISHOPSGATE
Founded Hand Alley
Removed to Broad St 1729-80

PRO (RG 4/4138, 4139) C 1705-53,

BLACKFRIARS
Founded 1662
Built Tothill St before 1667, Princes St
Westminster, 1703, Stamford St 1799,
1823-1962; Southwark 'near the Maese'
1666, St Thomas St 1703, united with
Stamford St 1823

DW (38.124; 201.7; 0D43); PRO
(RG 4/4489, 4513, 4535) C 1724-1833

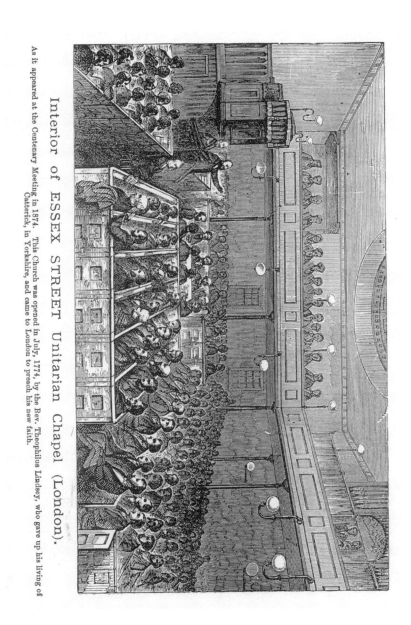

Interior of ESSEX STREET Unitarian Chapel (London).

As it appeared at the Centenary Meeting in 1874. This Church was opened in July, 1774, by the Rev. Theophilus Lindsey, who gave up his living of Catterick, in Yorkshire, and came to London to preach his new faith.

This building was pulled down in the late 1880's. The site is now occupied by Essex Hall,
the Headquarters of the Unitarian General Assembly.

FINSBURY
Glasshouse Yard GB, Worship St 1779
Bethnal Green /Winchmore Hill,
joined Baptist Union 1915

PRO (RG 4/4515) B 1785-1837, DW
(0D330/2, 317/2)

FINSBURY CIRCUS
Free Thinking Christians, Jewin St, circa
1818-50, *see* Battle Free Thinking
Christian Church

PRO (RG 4/4393) C 1824-1837

GOLDERS GREEN
Founded 1903 Weech Rd,
Child's Hill, Hoop Lane 1925

CH

GOODMANS FIELDS
GB Seventh Day, Mill Yard
Founded ?-1905

PRO (RG 4/4505,4506) C 1783-1837,
B 1732-33

GOODMANS FIELDS
Somerset Street

PRO (RG 4/4511,4512,4353) C 1758-
1811, B 1749-1826

HACKNEY
Paradise Fields. Founded 1665
Built Mare St 1668, Gravel Pit 1716,
New Gravel Pit MH 1858-1969

PRO (RG 4/4244) B 1812-37; DW
(burial register); Hackney Archives
Dept (D/E 237 GRA). The MIs have
been transcribed and printed (1880s);
the grave yard remains in existence.

HAMPSTEAD
Founded 1687
Built Red Lion Hill 1691, Rosslyn Hill 1862

CH; DW (38.127-38.192)

HIGHGATE HILL
Founded 1885
Built 1890-1961

DW

ISLINGTON
Founded 1671
Built MH Ct 1692, St Annes 1721, Little
Carter Lane, 1734 Upper St 1862, 1958

CH; DW; PRO (RG 4/4231, 4141)
C 1711-57,1760-1811

KENSINGTON
Founded 1774
Built Essex St Strand 1778, Palace Gardens
Terrace 1887, 1977

CH; DW (28.85); UC (D61); PRO
(RG 4/4488) C & B 1814-27; London
Guildhall L (MS 11936/257, 260);

KENTISH TOWN
Founded 1854
Built Clarence Rd 1855-1937

DW

KILBURN
Founded 1893
Built Quex Rd 1897, 1908-65

DW (OD48)

LIMEHOUSE
Elsa St. Founded 1884,
1895-1946

UC (D D Evans papers) A(2) 10.Built
Cup B(7)

LONDON
Barbican GB, *see also* Paul's Abbey

DW (38.73, 38.74, 38.77)

MARYLEBONE
Founded and built York St,
1824, Little Portland St
1833, University Hall, Gordon Sq 1909-13

DW (38.47-50; 38.100); St James's Sq
PRO (RG 4/ 4409) C 1825-37

MILES LANE
Cannon Street & Albion Chapel,
Moorgate, London Wall

PRO (RG 4/4405) C 1792-1837)

NEWINGTON GREEN
Founded 1686
Built 1708;

Hackney Archives Department
(D/E 257 NEW), DW

OLD JEWRY
Jewin St

PRO (RG 4/4408, 4349) C 1716-1819
B 1786-1787

PAUL'S ALLEY
GB – *see also* Barbican

DW (38.75)

SOUTH PLACE
Founded and built Parliament Ct,
Artillery St Bishopsgate; South Pl Finsbury
1824, Red Lion Sq, now South Place
Ethical Society;

PRO (RG 4/4393, 4369) C 1791-1811,
1824-37)

SOUTHWARK
Crutched Friars, King John Court

PRO (RG 4/4183, 4497) C 1729-1761

STEPNEY
Founded 1867
Built College Chapel, Stepney Green
1875-1946;

see A Causebrook, *College Chimes*
(about 1945)

STRATFORD
Founded 1857
Built West Ham Lane 1869

CH

WHITE'S ALLEY
GB

DW (38.85); London Guildhall L
(MS 592)

WOOD GREEN
Founded 1890
Built Newnham Rd, 1891-1966

DW

MIDDLESEX

ENFIELD
U Fellowship of Enfield and Barnet.
Founded 1963

CH

ENFIELD
Founded 1662, Baker St. MH

PRO (RG 4/1129) C 1727-37

FOREST GATE
Founded 1888
Built Upton Lane 1893, now meets elsewhere

CH

HAMMERSMITH
George Yard, Broadway, formerly
White Horse Chapel
Classified as Independent

PRO (RG 4/2203, 3593, 375) C1760-
1804, 1812-1837

UXBRIDGE
Founded 1717

PRO (RG 4/2332) C 1790-1836

NORFOLK

DISS
Founded 1697 (at Palgrave). Park Fields
1822-1954

PRO (RG 4/1263) C 1761-1836,
B 1797-1836

FILBY
Founded and built OM 1706-1940

Norfolk RO (FC2/15-23). The few
remaining MIs have been transcribed
(copy at Norfolk RO)

GREAT YARMOUTH
Founded 1644
Built OM Middlegate St, (Gaol St) 1845,
Greyfriars Way 1954

Norfolk RO (FC2)
PRO (RG 4/1399A, 1973, 2473) C
1706-1837, B 1785-1837
Middlegate United Reformed Church
Founded 1732 as a secession has early
records; others destroyed in WW2

HAPTON
Founded 1729
Built 1741-1959

PRO (RG 4/1255) C 1792-1830,
B 1808-1834

KINGS LYNN
Founded and built 1701 Spinner Lane, Broad Street, became Independent (moved 1838)

PRO (RG 4/2467, 1257, 1954, 2468, 2469) C 1745-1837

NORWICH
Founded 1662
Built St George's Colegate 1689,
Octagon Chapel 1756

Norfolk and Norwich RO (FC B); DW (95.34-5 Odgers)
PRO (RG 4/1965, 1966) C 1691-1837, B 1759-1837

NORTHAMPTONSHIRE

NORTHAMPTON
Founded 1827
Built King St 1828, Kettering Rd 1897,
Unitarian

Northampton RO; UC (C (1) 11)
PRO (RG 4/1141), C 1820-37

NORTHUMBERLAND

ALNWICK
Founded 1815, Ebenezer Unitarian Chapel, Correction House Yd – 1883

PRO (RG 4/1571) C 1817-31
DW (94.K1 Odgers)

ALNWICK
Sion Meeting House

PRO (RG 4/1349, 1697, 2679, 3417) C 1762-1837 DW (94.K1 Odgers)

BERWICK-on-TWEED
Golden Square

PRO (RG 4/1401) C 1834-1837

CHOPPINGTON
Founded and built Front St 1868-1975

Tyne and Wear Archive Services (with Newcastle Divine Unity Church records)

ETALL
Meeting House

PRO (RG 4/3214) circa 1777-1843

NEWCASTLE-UPON-TYNE

Founded 1662
Built Close Gate 1685, Hanover Sq 1727,
Church of Divine Unity, New Bridge St
1854, Ellison Place 1940

Northumberland RO (ZAN M 18/19);
DW (95.33 Odgers)
PRO (RG 4/1777) C 1752-1837; Tyne
and Wear ArchiveServices (1789)
Sheffield CL (UCR 257/3)

NEWCASTLE-UPON-TYNE

Pandon Bank. Unitarian Baptist, circa
1779-1836

Newcastle Public L; Newcastle Divine
Unity Church Records

NORTH SHIELDS

Founded eighteenth century,
Low Meeting – 1846

PRO (RG 4/3192) C 1756-1812;
UC (A(1)12), Tyne and Wear Archive
Services (1787)

NOTTINGHAMSHIRE

MANSFIELD

Founded 1666
Built OM Stockwell Gate, 1701

CH; Nottingham Univ Dept of
MSS (O1)
PRO (RG 4/1583, 2486), C 1738-
1837 B 1800-1811

NEWARK

Founded 1862
Built 1863 Kings Rd, 1884-1950;
see Nottingham High Pavement Chapel records

NOTTINGHAM

Founded 1860
Built Christ Church Peas Hill, 1864-1930

Nottingham Univ Dept of MSS
(Hi Z 1-16)

NOTTINGHAM

Founded 1662.
Built High Pavement 1691, 1805, 1876,
Lace Market 1982

RO, Nottingham Univ Dept of MSS
(Hi and Hi 2); UC (C53);
PRO (RG 4/137, 1587, 1588, 2674)
C 1690-1837)
NLW (Simon Jones Bequest);

NOTTINGHAM *contd.*

Nottinghamshire Family History Society Records Series vols. 53 and 74 contain indexes to family history records

NOTTINGHAM
Hyson Green. DM. Founded and built 22
Bentinck Road, 1883-1901

Nottingham Univ Dept of MSS
(Hi H 1-9)

OXFORDSHIRE

BANBURY
Founded 1672. GM Horsefair
Built 1716 Christ Church, 1850-1969,
reformed as a U Fellowship 1994

DW (38.45; 94K Odgers)
PRO (RG 4/1413) C 1816-37

BLOXHAM AND MILTON
Founded 1672
Built about 1700 (Bloxham).
Milton Chapel Lane, closed 1865

PRO (RG 4/1721) C 1789-1837

OXFORD
Society of Worshippers, Harris Manchester
College Founded 1957

CH

SHROPSHIRE

OLDBURY
Founded 1662. Hales Owen
Built 1708 Unity Pl 1806-1980

UC (C(1)11-12, C(1)42)
PRO (RG 4/1528, 1529, 1530, 2942,
2943) C 1715-45, 1759-1837

SHREWSBURY
Founded 1662
Built High St 1691; Shrewsbury PL

UC (C (1) 11)
PRO (RG 4/1818), C 1692-1837; NLW
(Astley papers) (Add MS 401A,
MS 603 Francis Tallents)

WEM

Founded before 1695
Built 1716 Noble St ?- 1874

PRO (RG 4/1533), C 1755-1836 & Deaths 1758-1833 *see* Shrewsbury records at RO

WHITCHURCH

Founded 1672
Built Broad Oak 1689, Doddington 1707-1844

PRO (RG 4/1414, 2496), C 1708-1724, 1743-1836, B 1746-1777, 1823-36

WHITCHURCH

Founded and built Church of the Saviour
Highgate, 1877-1921

see Shrewsbury records at RO

SOMERSET

ASHWICK

Founded before 1699
Built 1703, 1758-late nineteenth century

UC; PRO (RG 4/2052, 2345, 2346) C 1761-81, 1785-1837, B 1796-1836; Somerset RO

BATH

Founded 1672
Built Frog Lane 1692, Trim St 1795-1969;
Bath City RO; DW (94K4, 9 Odgers)

PRO (RG 4/55, 85, 2053, 2347, 2348, 2922) C 1719-1761, 1789-1837, B 1819-1837

BRIDGWATER

Founded 1662.
Built Christchurch Chapel, Dampier St 1688

Somerset RO and Osler family papers; PRO (RG 4/142) C 1755-1837, B 1833-35

BRISTOL

Clifton. Founded and built Oakfield Rd,
1864-1991; *see* Lewin's Mead and Brunswick Square.

BRISTOL

Founded 1662. Built Lewin's Mead 1694,
1791, Brunswick Square 1991

CH; Bristol RO; DW (OD 21-35); PRO (RG 4/1830, 2497, 3323, 3507), C 1718-1840, B 1768-1837

BRISTOL
Founded DM Montague St 1839.
Built 1861-1942

Somerset RO (D/N/wu 6/1)

CREWKERNE
Founded 1666.
Built Hermitage St 1733

PRO (RG 4/1547) C 1785-1836, B 1834; Somerset RO

ILMINSTER
Founded 1672
Built East St 1719

Somerset RO (D/N/ilm)
PRO (RG 4/1554, 3265) C 1718-1837, B 1786-1837

SHEPTON MALLET
Founded 1672
Built Cowl St 1696-1961; *see* Bristol, Lewin's Mead records

PRO (RG 4/2058, 2350, 2875) C 1757-1835, B 1802-37; Somerset RO

SOUTH PETHERTON
Old MH

PRO (RG 4/43, 2351, 4491) C 1694-1725, 1747-1770, 1786-1837, B 1821-1829

TAUNTON
GB Founded 1646
Built Mary St 1721; Somerset RO

PRO (RG 4/2937, 3324) C 1747-1837, B 1797-1837

TAUNTON
Founded and built Tancred St 1732-1815, united with Mary St Chapel

Somerset RO

YEOVIL
Founded 1660.
Built 1704, 1809, Vicarage St Kingston, 122 Goldcroft 1969

Somerset RO; PRO (RG 4/2933), C 1833, B 1833-36

STAFFORDSHIRE

BURSLEM
Circa 1822-47, *see* reference in Congleton
Chapel records under CHESHIRE

COSELEY
Sedgley OM. Founded 1662   CH; UC (C (1) 52); PRO (RG 4/3307)
Built 1717, 1875   C 1775-1837, B 1804-37

NEWCASTLE-UNDER-LYME
Founded 1672   CH; Tameside Local Studies L UC
Built 1694, 1717   (NU1/36/3q); (unlisted)

WALSALL
Founded 1662   CH; PRO (RG4/2582) C 1767-1837
Built 1700 High St 1715, Stafford St
1827-1980
Unitarian

WOLVERHAMPTON
Founded 1700   CH; PRO (RG 4/1426, 1878) C 1726-
Built 1701 John St, 1817 Snow Hill, 1831   1815, 1830-38
All Souls, Park Rd West 1911, now meeting
a Friends MH

SUFFOLK

BEDFIELD
Founded 1892.   CH
Built 1895

BURY ST EDMUNDS
Founded 1672.   Suffolk RO Bury St Edmunds
Built Church Gate St 1690, 1711   (ES/5/2.1) Suffolk RO Ipswich
                                (FK4/500/1) PRO (RG 4/38, 2059,
                                3923) C 1689-1836

FRAMLINGHAM

Founded 1660
Built 1717

CH. PRO (RG 4/1838, 1839, 3620) C 1710-1714, 1744-1837, B 1722-1770, 1792-1836

HAVERHILL

Old MH

PRO (RG 4/1844, 1845, 1794) C 1709-1839, B 1790-1814

IPSWICH

Founded 1672
Built OM House, St Nicholas St 1700

CH; Suffolk RO; PRO (RG 4/3197, 3622) C 1738-1837

SURREY

BRIXTON

Founded and built Effra Rd 1839, 1962

CH

CATFORD

Founded 1897
Built High St Lewisham 1910,
41 Bromley Rd Catford 1968

CH

CLAPHAM

South London Universalist Church,
Cavendish Rd, Founded ?-1951

Andover Harvard Theological L Cambridge MA USA (bMS 417 and bMS 369/ 36(12))

CROYDON

Founded 1880
Built Wellesley Rd, 1883 Friends Rd, 1958

CH

CROYDON

Founded 1886
Built DM Dennet Hall 1888-1931

Croydon CL

GODALMING

GB Founded 1783.
Built Meadrow 1789

CH; Surrey RO Guildford (141/1-33)

GUILDFORD
Founded 1874.
Built Ward St 1877-1972

Surrey RO Guildford (142/1-33). Godalming records have many Guildford references

HORLEY AND NUTFIELD
GB Founded 1668-1851

DW (38.84); UC (D7, D11)

PECKHAM
Founded 1875
Built Avondale Rd, 1882-1946

DW

PUTNEY
Founded 1882
Built East Hill, Wandsworth 1885,
205 Upper Richmond Rd, Putney 1985

see Richmond Church records

RICHMOND
Founded 1888
Built Ormond Rd; 1896

CH; Richmond Public Library

SUSSEX

BATTLE
Free Thinking Christians, circa 1818-50

DW (38.67; 38.87)

BATTLE
Founded 1780
Built Christ Church GM House,
1789-1836, 1840-98

E Sussex RO (NU3); UC (D9; D62) PRO (RG 4/1747) C 1789-1836, B 1791-93

BILLINGSHURST
GB Founded and built High St 1754

CH; DW (38.66); UC (D11) PRO (RG 4/2939) B 1821-36 registers and MIs have been transcribed (DW and CRO)

BRIGHTON
Founded 1797.
Built Jew St 1806, Cavendish St, 1812
New Road 1820

CH

CHICHESTER
Founded and built Eastgate 1671-1941
GB Boffin's Lane Fl 1680-1886 united
with Eastgate

West Sussex RO (BI/1/1-B1/9/7);
DW(38.86f OD 329. 4/5); PRO
(RG 4/2586, 2728) C 1730-1837

CUCKFIELD
GB. ?-1813

East Sussex RO (NU2 OM Ditchling
records); UC (MS title deeds 1802)
C (1)11, Cup C

DITCHLING
GB. Founded 1698
Built 1740

East Sussex RO (NU2); PRO
(RG 4/1796, 1797) C 1811-1833,
B 1821-37; Registers and MIs have
been transcribed (DW and CRO)

HASTINGS
Founded 1858, South Terrace 1868

CH; UC (C 12, C (1) 42)

HORSHAM
GB Founded 1648
Built Worthing Rd 1721

West Sussex RO (B2); DW (38.86);
UC (D9; D11); PRO (RG 4/2062, 2729)
C 1688, 1706-1836, B 1721-68, 1771-
1837); registers and MIs have been
transcribed (DW and RO)

LEWES
Founded 1662
Built Westgate 1687, 1700

CH; East Sussex RO (NU1); UC (D61)

LEWES
GB Founded 1741 Eastport Lane united with
Westgate Chapel 1818,

see East Sussex RO
(NU2 Ditchling)

NORTHIAM
GB Founded 1796 .Built Herman Hill 1810

E Sussex RO; UC (D62); *see also* Kent and Sussex U Christian Association

TURNERS HILL
see Horley and Nutfield under SURREY

WORTHING
U Fellowship Founded 1964

CH

WARWICKSHIRE

ALCESTER
Founded before 1693, Knowsley Rd
Old Chapel 1721-1896

Warwickshire RO (CR 1018); PRO (RG 4/3367) C 1774-1836, Deaths 1777-1834, RG 8/96, C 1749-1773

ATHERSTONE
OM. Founded 1689
Built Long St 1725-1918

PRO (RG 4/2367) C 1765-94

BIRMINGHAM
Founded 1672
Built 1692 New Meeting House, Moor St, 1732, 1802 Church of Messiah, Broad St, 1862, Unitarian New Meeting Ryland St 1973

CH; Birmingham RL; PRO (RG 4/2948, 3112, 3633, 3634, 3635) C 1719, 1735-1840, B not dated

BIRMINGHAM
Church of the Saviour. Founded and built 1847-95

Birmingham RL (258925; 259532; 260167 George Dawson Collection; 264036)

BIRMINGHAM
Hollywood. Founded 1670
Built Kingswood (Dollax) 1708, 1793

CH; Birmingham RL (303437)

BIRMINGHAM
Founded 1834
Built Newhall Hill 1840, Gibson Rd, Handsworth 1951, services suspended

Birmingham RL copy of J Stych, *History of Newhall Hill Church,* (1892) contains MS notes

BIRMINGHAM
OM. Founded 1687
Built 1689, 1795, 1885-1950

Birmingham RL (258256); DW (38. 123); UC (C11.C142)
PRO (RG 4/1430, 1431, 2945, 2946, 2947, 3368) C 1774-1838, M 1811-1838, B 1784-1858. C H Beale, *Memorials OMH and Burial Grounds* (1882), gives full transcription & notes

BIRMINGHAM
Founded and built Paradise St about 1790, Little Cannon St 1809-14
Unitarian

PRO (RG4/1758) C 1791-1813

BIRMINGHAM
Small Heath. Founded 1893
Built Waverley Rd Church 1898

CH; *see also* Birmingham Church of the Saviour

COVENTRY
GM. Founded 1662
Built Smithfield St 1700
Holyhead Rd 1937

CH; Coventry City RO (Acc 137; 460; 480-481); DW (94K12 Odgers); UC (C (1) 11 and (2) 6)
PRO (RG4/2950, 2951) C 1717-1819, 1821-37; NLW (MS 4844E)

KENILWORTH
Founded and built Rosemary Hill about 1705, 1846-91

Warwickshire RO (HR 31); PRO (RG4/3060), C 1818-32

TAMWORTH
Founded 1690
Built Colehill now Victoria Rd 1724, services suspended

CH; PRO (RG4/2979, 3758A) C 1695-1837, B 1822-36

WARWICK
Founded 1691
Built High St 1780

CH; Warwickshire RO (CR 860); UC (C 42); PRO (RG 4/2808, C 1790-1837)

WEST BROMWICH
Founded 1871
Built Lodge Rd 1875-1979, services suspended

Smethwick PL

WESTMORELAND

KENDAL
Founded 1687
Built Market Place 1720

Cumbria RO Kendal (WDFCN);
DW (95.23 Odgers; UC D81);
PRO (RG 4/2896, 3042) C 1687-183
B 1755-1834

WILTSHIRE

CALNE
Founded 1662-1831

Somerset RO (D/N/wu 4); Wiltshire
RO (1241/29 and 37)

DEVIZES
Founded 1670-1867

PRO (RG 4/2231) C 1781-1836,
B 1792-1837

NEW SARUM
Salt Lane

PRO (RG 4/3118), C1723-1785

RUSHALL
GB Founded and built 1706-1972

DW (OB 329/1); Wiltshire RO
(1332/1-29)

SWINDON
U Fellowship Founded 1961

CH

TROWBRIDGE
GB Founded 1655.
Built before 1714, Conigree Chapel 1857

Wiltshire RO (1241, 1476, 2215);
Trowbridge UDC Lansdown
Collection for papers re. Samuel
Martin; PRO (RG 4/2958) C 1816-37

TROWBRIDGE
Presbyterian; Silver Street

PRO (RG 4/2597) C 1757-1837, B 1782-1837

WARMINSTER
Founded 1687
Built OM North Row, 1704-1869

Wiltshire RO; DW (95.45-6 Odgers); PRO (RG 4/3768A) C 1762-1836

WORCESTERSHIRE

BEWDLEY
Founded 1696
Built High St 1696/70-1894

PRO (RG 4/2959) C 1744-1823, B 1812-15, Deaths 1789, Ma 1780

CRADLEY
Founded and built 1707, Pensnet Meadows 1716, Netherend Chapel, Park Lane 1796;

CH; PRO (RG 4/1907, 2015) C 1789-1837, B 1761-1826

DUDLEY
Founded 1690
Built Wolverhampton St 1702, 1717

CH; UC (C(1) 11, C (1) 52, C (2) 6); PRO (RG 4/2736, 3477) C 1726, 1743-72,1775-1837, B 1831-35

EVESHAM
Founded 1690.
Built Oat St 1737

CH; Hereford and Worcester RO (898.4; f898.8); PRO (RG 4/3373) C 1778-1837, B 1822-36; NLW, Diary of Timothy Davies; UC (unlisted).

KIDDERMINSTER
NM House. Founded 1781
Built Church St 1782

CH; Hereford and Worcester RO (898.4)
PRO (RG 4/2738), C 1783-1836. E P Prime, *History* (Kidderminster, 1900), contains selected MIs and other lists; UC (C (1) 11)

LYE
Founded 1790 CH
Built High St 1806, 1861

STOURBRIDGE
Founded and built Coventry St, 1698   Hereford and Worcester RO (b 898.4;
High St 1788   898.4; s 898.4)

YORKSHIRE

BOLTON-ON-DEARNE
Founded and built Priory Rd 1911-72   Sheffield CL

BRADFORD
Founded and built Broadway Ave 1906   CH

BRADFORD
Founded 1672   CH; Bradford District Archives Dept
Built Toad Lane 1719, Chapel Lane 1869, (B929.SBLA; DB39/27/4; 30D81;
Russell St 1971   31D81; 44D88; DB39/44/1-2;
                                       Strongroom 81); Shrewsbury PL
                                       (Astley papers 1067/ 181-182. 186);
                                       NLW (MSS 315t-87) E Ceredig Jones
                                       MSS; PRO (RG 4/1702, 2372, 2633)
                                       C 1730-1767, 1785-1837, B 1786-1836

DEWSBURY
Founded 1858   Yorkshire U Union records; *see* Leeds
Built Willans Rd 1866-1953   Mill   Hill   Chapel   records

DONCASTER
Founded 169   CH; Sheffield CL (LD 1162-1164) UC
Built Hallgate 1744, 1912   (197 (4), 250 (8-9))

ELLAND
Founded 1685   PRO (RG 4/2641) C 1741-1816,
Built Southgate Chapel 1697, Christ   B 1745-1813; Leeds Mill Hill Chapel
Church, Huddersfield Rd 1866-1914   records (90); *see* Yorkshire Unitarian
                                       Union records

HALIFAX

Founded 1672
Built 1696 Northgate End Chapel 1872-1979

Calderdale Archives Dept; Shrewsbury PL (Astley papers 1067); PRO (RG 4/3167, 3348) C 1747-1837, B 1812-37; UC (unlisted)

HUDDERSFIELD

Founded 1846
Built Fitzwilliam St 1854-76, New North Road 1962-73

Leeds Mill Hill Chapel Records (86a), *see* Yorkshire Unitarian Union records

IDLE

Founded 1853
Built Highfield Rd 1858-1918

Yorkshire Unitarian Union Records. Leeds Mill Hill Chapel records (89a)

KINGSTON-UPON-HULL

Founded 1662
Built Bowl Alley Lane before 1700, Park St 1824, 1978

CH; Hull City RO; PRO (RG 4/143, 3752, 4490) C 1705-55, 1750-1881, 1828-35

KINGSTON-UPON-HULL

Unitarian Baptist Founded about 1807

PRO (RG 4/4483) C 1807-12

LEEDS

Holbeck DM 1844
Built Domestic St 1883-1929

Leeds Mill Hill Chapel records (78-85)

LEEDS

Hunslet. Founded 1863
Built Joseph St 1868-1970

Leeds Mill Hill Chapel Records (94)

LEEDS

Founded 1662.
Built Mill Hill 1674, 1848;

CH; PRO (RG 4/3138, 3675, 3724), C 1650-1716, 1720-1837, B & Deaths 1693-1716, 1754-1837

MALTON, NEW
Founded and built Wheelgate 1715-1952

North Yorkshire RO (R/1/ML); Yorkshire U Union; PRO (RG 4/2077, 2657) C 1770-1837, B 1778-1836

MEXBOROUGH
Founded 1912
Built College Rd 1913

CH; Sheffield CL (UCR 68/46)

MIDDLESBROUGH
Founded 1833
Built 1873-1970, Christ Church, Corporation Rd

Teeside archives

NEW MILL
Lydgate. Founded 1671
Built 1695, 1768

PRO (RG 4/3671) C 1743-1840
B 1700-1840
Yorkshire Unitarian Union records UC (C(1)11)

PUDSEY
Founded 1853
Built Church Lane 1861

CH; Leeds Mill Hill Chapel records (86b)

ROTHERHAM
Founded 1662
Built 1706 Church of Our Father,
Moorgate Street 1880-1986

PRO (RG 4/2195, 2196, 3206) C 1746-1836, B 1819-25); Sheffield CL (LD 1162-1164); Rotherham CL Archives (204/N); UC (281/3); W Blazeby, Rotherham OMH (1906), includes a transcription of the registers 1748-1837

SCARBOROUGH
Founded 1873
Built Westborough Rd 1877

CH; Leeds Mill Hill Chapel Records (86), Sheffield CL (UCR 197/4)

SELBY
Founded 1672
Built St Michael's Chapel, Millgate 1699,
1903-68

Wakefield MD Archives; PRO (RG 4/3178) C 1797-1836, & Deaths 1836 *see* Yorkshire Unitarian Union records

SHEFFIELD
Attercliffe. Founded 1901
Built Shirland Lane 1906-71

Sheffield CL (UCR)

SHEFFIELD
Crookesmoor. Founded 1859
Built Upperthorpe 1861, Crookesmoor Rd
1915-82

Sheffield CL (UCR)

SHEFFIELD
Fulwood. Founded 1714
Built Whiteley Lane 1728
Classed as Independent

CH; Sheffield CL (M.D. 1400-1416
UCR 79/4-28; L.C.64; LD 1162-1164);
PRO (RG 4/3179) C 1820-37

SHEFFIELD
Norfolk St. Founded 1660
Built 1678, 1700 Upper Chapel

CH; Sheffield CL (HD 29; LD 162-64)
PRO (RG 4/2085, 2197, 2198, 3207,
4482) C 1681-1837, B 1745-1837;
J E Manning, *History* (Sheffield,
1900), includes a transcription of the
registers

SHEFFIELD
Stannington. Founded and built Underbank
Chapel 1652, 1742

CH; Sheffield CL (RC 230/1-9 LC
164); Wakefield MD Archives (re.
Lower Bradfield School); PRO
(RG 4/2768, 4110), C 1718-1837

SHELF
Pepper Hill. Founded 1858
Built 1862, 1936

CH; Yorkshire Unitarian Union records

STAINFORTH
Founded and built 1816-1865
Unitarian

PRO (RG 4/4051) C 1818-35

THORNE
Founded and built Canal St (Orchard St)
1816 - late nineteenth century. *Unitarian*

PRO (RG 4/3080) C and B 1817-37

TODMORDEN
Founded 1818
Built Hanging Ditch 1824, Fielden Sq
1869-1992

CH; UC (Cup D)

WAKEFIELD
Founded 1662
Built Westgate 1697, 1752

CH; Wakefield Metropolitan District
Archives; PRO (RG 4/2779, 3704)
C 1761-1837, B 1785-1835);
UC (A (1) 14).

WELBURN
Founded 1819
Built 1825-62

North Yorkshire RO (R/1/ML2) *see*
Wheelgate Chapel, Malton records;
Christian Reformer (1840), p.610

WHITBY
Cliff Lane Chapel

PRO (RG 4/3934) circa 1789-1837

WHITBY
Founded 1694
Built Flowergate 1750

North Yorkshire RO; DW (38.119 3);
PRO (RG 4/2020) C and B 1695-1832,
Ma 1695-1710

YORK
Founded 1692
Built St Savioursgate 1693

CH; Univ York Borthwick Inst;
PRO (RG 4/3780) C 1721-1836)
UC (Cupboard 4) B 1794-1837

ISLE OF MAN

DOUGLAS
Founded 1880
Built 1884-97

U Fellowship 1977;CH

Congregations in Scotland

ABERDEEN
Founded 1835
Built George St. 1840
Skene Street, 1906

CH; Strathclyde Regional Archives

(TD 983/2/1/1-3)

DUNDEE
Founded 1785
Built Constitution Hill 1870,
Dudhope St 1969

Dundee Archives Centre; Strathclyde
Regional Archives (TD 983/2/2/1-4)

EDINBURGH
Founded 1776
Built Young St 1823, St Mark's Castle
Terrace 1835

CH; Scottish RO (CH 15/1); DW
(24.80); UC (CI 52)

EDINBURGH
U Fellowship. Founded 1952-74

Scottish RO (CH 15/2)

GIRVAN
Wilson St Founded and built 1850-63

Scottish RO (CH 15/1/45)

GLASGOW
Founded 1791
Built Union St 1812, St Vincent 1856-74,
Berkeley St 1974

Strathclyde Regional Archives,
Mitchell Library (TO 978/1-17)

GLASGOW
Calton. Founded 1871
Built South St, Mungo St, Ross St 1876-1947

Strathclyde Regional Archives;
Mitchell Library (TD 978/18-21)

KIBARCHAN
Founded 1887
Built New St 1891-1900

Strathclyde Regional Archives
(TD 383)

KILMARNOCK
Founded 1795
Built Clerk's Lane 1885. Closed circa 1930

Strathclyde Regional Archives (TD 383)

KIRKCALDY

Founded 1890
Built 1899-1920, see Glasgow St
Vincent St records

Strathclyde Regional Archives

PAISLEY

Founded 1823
Built George St. Closed circa 1900

see Glasgow, St Vincent St records,
Strathclyde Regional Archives (TD 383)

PERTH

Built North William St 1876-85

Strathclyde Regional Archives
(TD 983/1/5/1).

STENHOUSEMUIR

St Paul's Universalist Church. Founded 1867
Built 1875-1929; many references in
Dundee Chapel records

Note: There are numerous references to congregations, including those not listed here, in
Scottish Unitarian Association Archives – *see* Strathclyde Regional Archives (TD 383)

Congregations in Wales

BRECONSHIRE

LLANAFANFAWR
Troedrhiwdalar Chapel (Presbyterian)   PRO (RG 4/3050) C 1804-1837

LLANDOVALLY
Bechfa Chapel (Presbyterian)   PRO (RG 4/3921) C 1760, 1767, 1801-
                                      1837. B 1805-1836

LLANWORTYD
Gelynos Chapel (Presbyterian)   PRO (RG 4/3051) C 1800-1837)

CARMARTHENSHIRE

CAPEL IFAN
Panteg. Founded 1697   CH
Built 1764, 1900

CARMARTHEN
Founded and built 1812, Park-y-Velvet   CH; NLW (MS 4457E)
Mansel St, 1849-1992

CWMMARDHU
Founded 1790   Carmarthen RO (MS 6457) NLW (MS
Built 1832, now a Unitarian Youth Hostel   4457E)

CARDIGANSHIRE

ABERYSTWYTH
MH Founded 1902, New Street   NLW (Deposit 1304A-1305A)
Built 1902-78

ALLTYBLACA
Founded and built 1740, 1837   CH

CELLAN
Caeronnen. Founded and built 1672, 1846   CH; NLW (MS 3500B)

CILIAU AERON
Founded and built 1689, 1755, 1899   CH

CRIBYN
Founded and built 1790, 1852   CH

CWMSYCHBANT
Capel-y-Cwm. Founded 1896   CH
Built 1906

CWRTNEWYDD
Capel-y-Bryn. Founded 1836   CH
Built 1882

FELINFACH
Rhydygwin. Founded 1802   CH
Built 1848

LAMPETER
Founded 1874   CH
Built 1876 Brondeifi, 1903

LAMPETER
Founded 1801   CH
Built Ystrad 1802, Capel-y-Groes
Llanwen 1890

LLANDYSUL
Founded and built Graig 1868, 1884   CH; list of members 1868 in Yr.
                                              Ymofyndd, vol.28, p.225

PONTISAN
Llwynrhydowen. Founded and built 1726,   CH; NLW (MSS 43618, 4844E)
1733, 1791, 1834, 1879

PRENGWYN
Pantydefaid. Founded 1801 CH
Built 1802, 1836

ST CLEARS
GB Founded and built 1799-1892 NLW (Deposit 647A; MS 4457E)

TALGARREG
Capel-y-Fadfa. Founded 1812 CH
Built 1813, 1906

DENBIGHSHIRE

WREXHAM
Founded 1659. Chester St – Closed PRO (RG 4/3446, 4131, 4421) C 1713-
nineteenth century 19, 1743-1837, B 1746-1837

FLINTSHIRE

NEWMARKET
The Old or John Wynne's Chapel PRO (RG 4/3947) C 1796-1837

GLAMORGAN

ABERDARE
Founded and built Highland Place, CH
Monk St 1860

BLAENGWRACH
Founded and built at Glynneath – 1878 NLW (MS 1144D)

BRIDGEND
Founded 1672 NLW (MS 7968B)
Built 1715-20 Park St 1795

CARDIFF
Founded 1880   CH
Built West Grove 1887

CARDIFF
St Fagans Founded 1756   NLW (MS 4457E)
Built Penrhiw, Drefach, Llandysul 1777 - mid-
nineteenth century re-erected Welsh National
Folk Museum, St Fagans. Archive of Welsh
National Folk Museum, Cardiff

CEFN COED YCYMMER
Founded and built 1747 Hen Dy Cwrdd,   CH; Glamorgan Archive Service (D/D
Old Chapel Rd 1853   Uni 1/1-45)

CWMBACH
Founded 1857   *see* Aberdare Highland Place Chapel
Built 1859 Bridge St, Abernantygroes   records
1879-1946,

GELLIONNEN
Llangyfelach. Founded 1692   NLW (MSs 4364B) PRO (RG 4/3884,
Built 1695, 1801 as Trebanos   4415) C 1763-1798, 1806-1814, B 1786

MERTHYR TYDFIL
Founded 1814. Twyn-yr-odyn   PRO (RG 4/3498) C 1804-36
Built 1820 Thomas St 1901-1968

MERTHYR TYDFIL
Founded 1749, Ynysgau. Closed   PRO (RG 4/4090) C 1786-1837
nineteenth century

NEATH
Green St circa 1854; deeds only known to exist

NOTTAGE
GB Founded and built 1789, 1877   CH

PONTYPRIDD
Founded 1801. Built 1802, 1836-1976   Pontypridd RL

SWANSEA
Founded 1662

Built 1689 High St, 1847, rebuilt 1991

CH; PRO (RG 4/3665, 4096) C 1753-1792, 1814-1837, B 1783-1784, 1814-1837

SWANSEA
GB. Founded and built 1689-1852

W Glamorgan Area RO Swansea (DB 40/1-4)

TREBANOS
Founded 1862

Built Graig 1894

CH

TRECYNON
Founded and built 1751 Hen Dy Cwrdd, Alma St 1862

CH; NLW (MSS 4361-70 and 14, 147-14, 213 Rees Jenkin Jones MSS)

TREORCHY
Glanrhondda. Founded 1893

Built 1895

CH

WICK
GB Founded and built 1792

CH

Other bodies

BOLTON DISTRICT MISSIONARY ASSOCIATION

UC (C (1) 37)

BOLTON DISTRICT UNITARIAN DISTRICT ASSOCIATION

UC (C (1) 36)

BRITISH AND FOREIGN UNITARIAN ASSOCIATION

DW, Somerset RO (DD/X/LV) correspondence with Western Union 1825-34 New York PL (MSS 68-1080) 6 folders of correspondence 1825- 67

CARMARTHENSHIRE UNITARIAN CHAPELS	NLW (MS 4457E) Schedules and notes of deeds and documents twentieth century
CHESHIRE CLASSIS	Brook St Chapel Knutsford minutes 1691-1745: UC (C (2)3)
DEVON AND CORNWALL UNITARIAN ASSOCIATION	George's M Exeter papers and one vol. 1814-30
DEVON AND CORNWALL UNITED MINISTERS	From 1707. UC (C (2) 3 and unlisted)
DUDLEY DOUBLE LECTURE	Birmingham RL (Unitarian NM records 156) ministers 1855-57, note book on lectures c.1723-c.1854
EAST CHESHIRE UNION OF UNITARIAN AND FREE CHURCHES	Tameside Local Studies L (NU1/1-74)
EAST KENT GENERAL BAPTIST CHURCHES	DW (38.72; 38.79a; 38.80) journals and minutes 1717-1809
EAST AND WEST KENT GENERAL BAPTIST CHURCHES	DW (38.79b) records 1768-1819
EASTERN UNION OF UNITARIAN AND FREE CHRISTIAN CHURCHES	Norfolk and Norwich RO (FC 7/1) minutes 1813-59; (FC 13/83) accounts 1813-63
EXETER ASSEMBLY	Devon RO, minutes 1655-59, 1721/2-1923; DW (38.24; 38.28) minutes 1721-28. UC(unlisted)
FREE THINKING CHRISTIANS	At Battle, Jewin St, London, Cranbrook Dewsbury, Loughborough and Philadelphia (USA); DW (38.67; 38.87)

GENERAL BAPTIST ASSEMBLY	DW, papers from 1689
GENERAL BAPTIST CHURCHES	UC (D10) Notes and extracts from books and documents Burgess MSS
KENT AND SUSSEX GENERAL BAPTIST CHURCHES	DW (38.83)
KENT AND SUSSEX UNITARIAN CHRISTIAN ASSOCIATION	DW, UC (D62); E Sussex RO (NU4/3/5)
LANCASHIRE AND CHESHIRE CHRISTIAN ASSOCIATION	Liverpool RO (288 ULL/8/6) objects and rules 1919. UC (A18)
LANCASHIRE FIRST PRESBYTERIAN CLASSIS	John Rylands University Library of Manchester minutes 1646-60
LIVERPOOL DISTRICT MISSIONARY UC ASSOCIATION	Liverpool RO (Acc 2609; 2B8ULL) minutes 1914-61; (B(1)12 and B(1)42)
LIVERPOOL DISTRICT SUNDAY SCHOOL UNION	Liverpool RO (288 ULL; Acc 3308)
LONDON AND SOUTH EASTERN COUNTIES PROVINCIAL ASSEMBLY OF NON-SUBSCRIBING MINISTERS AND CONGREGATIONS	DW (12 modern folios) papers nineteenth-twentieth century
LONDON AND SOUTHERN GENERAL BAPTIST ASSOCIATION	DW (38.82; 38.86) minutes 1832-45
LONDON (UNITARIAN) LAYMEN'S CLUB	DW (24.177) minutes and accounts 1903-60
MANCHESTER DISTRICT ASSOCIATION OF UNITARIAN AND FREE CHRISTIAN CHURCHES	UC Collection

MANCHESTER SUNDAY SCHOOL UNION/ASSOCIATION	UC Collection
MIDLAND SUNDAY SCHOOL ASSOCIATION	Birmingham RL (Unitarian NM records 167-8) 1931-53
MONTHLY MEETING OF PROTESTANT DISSENTING MINISTERS OF WARWICKSHIRE AND NEIGHBOURING COUNTIES	Birmingham RL (Unitarian NM records 88-9; 90-94; 169) minutes etc 1782-1939
NEWCASTLE AND DISTRICT UNITARIAN CHRISTIAN ASSOCIATION	Newcastle Church of the Divine Unity minutes 1879-1958
NON-CON CLUB	DW (28.62-3) minutes 1828-52
NOTTINGHAM PRESBYTERIAN CLASSIS	Nottingham Univ Dept of MSS (Hi2/M/1) minutes 1654-60
NORTH LANCASHIRE AND WESTMORLAND UNITARIAN ASSOCIATION	Lancashire RO (DDX 207/5); Bath CL (NUL6)
PRESBYTERIAN COLLEGE CARMARTHEN	NLW (MSS 10325-30B)
PRESBYTERIAN MINISTERS OF DERBYSHIRE, NOTTINGHAMSHIRE AND SOUTH YORKSHIRE	Nottingham Univ Dept of MSS (Hi/V/21) minutes 1798-1856
PROVINCIAL ASSEMBLY OF LANCASHIRE AND CHESHIRE	Manchester CL Archives Dept (L62) 1875-1971; Liverpool RO (288H0P/ 5/1-3; 288ULL/8/8/1-3) meetings in Liverpool nineteenth century; NLW (MS 13672); UC (C(2)3, C(1) 11, C (2) 9. Cupboard B)
SCOTTISH MISSION (UNIVERSALIST)	Andover-Harvard L Cambridge MA USA 12-page anonymous MS history

SCOTTISH UNITARAN ASSOCIATION	Strathclyde Regional Archives (TD 583)
SOUTH WALES UNITARIAN SOCIETY	NLW (MS 13145A)
SOUTHERN UNITARIAN ASSOCIATION	Portsmouth RO
UNITARIAN COLLEGE MANCHESTER	UC Collection
WARRINGTON CLASSIS	Liverpool RO (288 ULL/8/1-3) minutes 1719-22; Shrewsbury PL (Astley papers 1067/134) meeting of 18 May 1762
WELSH UNITARIAN MINISTERS EDUCATION FUND	NLW (Simon Jones Bequest)
WEST RIDING MEETING OF MINISTERS	Leeds Mill Hill Chapel (91) I 844-63 with preface re. 1691-97
WESTERN UNITARIAN SOCIETY	DW (OD.33) 1805-66
WESTERN UNION MINISTERS MEETING	Somerset RO (D/N/wu 3/1) minutes 1862-64, 1908-33
WESTERN UNION OF UNITARIAN AND FREE CHRISTIAN CHURCHES	Somerset RO (D/N/wu; DO/X/LV: D/N/mst, tau/6/7) records 1792-1957
WIDOWS FUND OF LANCASHIRE AND CHESHIRE	Manchester CL Archives Dept (M287)
WILLASTON SCHOOL	Cheshire RO (at Chester)
YORKSHIRE UNITARIAN SUNDAY SCHOOL UNION	Leeds Mill Hill Chapel (92) minutes 1894-1921
Yr Ymofynnydd	(The Journal of Welsh-Speaking Unitarianism, founded 1918) NLW (Simon Jones Bequest)

Non-Subscribing Presbyterian Church of Ireland

These are records of the following congregations and associated organisations in the Public Record Office of Northern Ireland, 66 Balmoral Avenue, Belfast BT9 6NY in the CR/4 series

BALLEE
Old Presbyterian MH. Founded 1697
Built 1721, 1890
(MIC 1B/3A register 1811-1985)

BALLYCARRY
Founded Presbyterian Church 1646
Built Main St. 1871

BALLYCLARE
Founded MH 1646
Built Main St 1871

BANBRIDGE
First Presbyterian NS Cong
Founded and built 1716
Downshire Rd 1844

BELFAST
Second Presbyterian Cong
Founded and built 1708
Elmwood Ave 1896

BELFAST
DM Founded 1853
Built 1864 destroyed by fire

BELFAST
First Presbyterian Church
Founded 1644
Built 1688, 1708 Rosemary St 1783

CLOUGH
NS Presbyterian Church
Founded 1829 Built 1837

COMBER
NS Presbyterian Church Founded 1836
Built Mill St 1838

DOWN PATRICK
First Presbyterian Church Founded 1650
Built Stream St 1710

DROMORE
First NS Presbyterian Church
Founded 1622 Built Rampart St 1801

DONMURRY
NS Church founded 1676
Built 1714 Glebe 1779

KILLINCHY
NS Presbyterian Church Founded
and built 1670, 1846

MONEYREAGH
NS Presbyterian Church Founded 1719
Built 1770

NEWRY
First Presbyterian NS Church.
Founded 1650
Built 1688 John Mitchell Race 1853

NEWTOWNARDS
First Presbyterian Congregation.
Founded 1642
Built 1724 Victoria Ave 1924

RADEMON
NS Presbyterian Church (First Kilmore)
Founded 1713
Built 1715, 1787

TEMPLPATRICK
Presbyterian Church Founded 1646
Built 1670, 1881

WARRENPOINT
First Presbyterian Church (Remonstrant)
Founded and built 1707 Burren Rd 1820

Other bodies

DOWN AND ANTRIM UNITARIAN CHRISTIAN ASSOCIATION

FREE CONGREGATIONAL UNION (IRELAND)

NON-SUBSCRIBING PRESBYTERIAN CHURCH OF IRELAND

NORTHERN PRESBYTERY OF ANTRIM

PRESBYTERY OF ARMAGH

UNITARIAN SOCIETY FOR THE DIFFUSION OF CHRISTIAN KNOWLEDGE